Audel Water Well Pumps and Systems Mini-Ref

R. Dodge Woodson

WILEY

John Wiley & Sons, Inc.

Published by John Wiley & Sons, Inc., Hoboken, New Jersey

Published simultaneously in Canada

For general information about our other products and services, please contact our Customer Care Department within the United States at (800) 762-2974, outside the United States at (317) 572-3993 or fax (317) 572-4002.

Wiley also publishes its books in a variety of electronic formats. Some content that appears in print may not be available in electronic books. For more information about Wiley products, visit our web site at www.wiley.com.

Library of Congress Cataloging-in-Publication Data:

Woodson, R. Dodge (Roger Dodge), 1955–
    Audel water well pumps and systems mini-ref / R. Dodge Woodson.
      pages cm.—(Audel technical trades series)
    Includes index.
    ISBN 978-1-118-11480-3 (pbk.); 978-1-118-17024-3 (ebk); 978-1-118-17025-0 (ebk); 978-1-118-17027-4 (ebk); 978-1-118-17028-1 (ebk); 978-1-118-17029-8 (ebk)
    1. Wells—Handbooks, manuals, etc. 2. Wells—Maintenance and repair—Handbooks, manuals, etc. 3. Pumping machinery—Handbooks, manuals, etc. I. Title.
    TD405.W65 2012
    621.2′52–dc23
                                    2011045252

CONTENTS

Chapter 9 SUBMERSIBLE PUMP INSTALLATION 101

Chapter 10 BOOSTER PUMPS 109

Chapter 11 WATER QUALITY 119

Chapter 12 TROUBLESHOOTING AND REPAIRS

125

Appendix: ADDITIONAL INFORMATION AND RESOURCES

161

TYPES OF WELLS

There are many types of wells in use, and the type that is chosen by a builder, home owner, or architect is often determined by local conditions. For example, shallow wells are not always an option. And when they are, they may not be the best choice. Drilled wells can be used in all building plans, but they are expensive. This can be a drawback.

Pump selection often depends on the type of well the pump will serve. A submersible pump can be used in a shallow well, but it rarely is. A single-pipe jet pump is not suitable for installation with a deep well. It is important to install the right pump for the job. To do this, you must understand wells and the requirements associated with them.

DUG WELLS

Dug wells were very common a hundred years ago. They are still used occasionally in today's building world, but they are rare. A dug well is used when ground conditions allow the well to be dug to a suitable depth. Most of these wells range in depth from 20 to 35 feet. Deeper wells are possible, but the deeper they are, the more difficult it is to keep them from caving in.

As a young plumber I worked with dug wells in Virginia. Back then the piping installed in the well was galvanized steel. The process required to remove such piping was labor intensive. It was not possible to attach the piping to a motorized reel and wind it up out of the well. We had to set up a tripod and lift the heavy steel piping up, section by section, until we could secure a portion of it in the tripod. Then we would use pipe wrenches to unscrew the threaded joints. We repeated the process until the last piece of piping was out of the well. That was hard, heavy work.

The dug wells I used to work on were lined with rocks. Brave—or stupid—plumbers would sometimes use the rock walls to climb down into the wells. I never did that, but on two occasions I watched another plumber do it. He put his back against one wall and placed his feet on the rocks used to secure the opposite side of the well. Little by little he wiggled his way down into the well. The rocks were damp and slippery, and it was not uncommon for snakes to inhabit the rock lining. To say the least, this was hard-core plumbing.

It has been more than 30 years since I worked with a dug well, but they still exist. I know where three such wells exist in Maine today, in spite of the fact that much of Maine is too rocky or sandy to support dug wells. Many of them have been decommissioned and replaced with drilled wells.

Dug wells are generally shallow and have a diameter of 3 to 4 feet. They are not a great water source. First of all, they can run dry when there is a lack of rain. When they are in operation it is fairly common for them to become contaminated. All in all, dug wells can be used as a water supply for livestock, but they should not be considered a viable option for a modern plumbing system.

SHALLOW WELLS

Shallow wells are a more modern cousin of dug wells. These wells are constructed by boring, adhering to the same principles that were used for dug wells. Instead of rock walls being used to support them, preformed concrete sections line modern shallow wells. Sections of concrete are positioned in the well so that they stack on top of each other.

Once the concrete casing is installed it must be grouted to prevent groundwater from entering the well. Surface water and water near the ground surface can contaminate a well, which is why grouting is so important. A large concrete cover is placed over the well casing once all well and pump work is completed. The cover is sized to fit the casing that rises to a point above ground level. Gravity holds the cover in place.

Because of the limited depth of a shallow well there is a risk that it will not maintain a suitable water level during dry weather conditions. As a home builder in Virginia I had many shallow wells installed. They normally worked fine. But there were some hot, dry summers when the water table dropped to a point where the wells had difficulty recovering from use. There was basically nothing that could be done about this situation. It is possible to haul potable water in by truck and fill the well, but I can't recall this ever being done.

Another problem that I have seen with shallow wells is that, over time, they can fill in with sand. There is space below the concrete casing that can allow sand to seep into the well, which causes problems in the plumbing system.

Sand that builds up in a well can come through the water service piping and enter the water distribution system. Obviously, nobody wants sand in their drinking water. The grit does a lot of damage to the fittings, pumps, faucets, and fixtures in a plumbing system.

If a shallow well is deep enough, the drop pipe that contains the foot valve can be shortened when sand invades the well. This raises the level of the foot valve and gets it out of the sand. If a builder suspects sandy soil, then a drilled well is a better option than a shallow well.

Aquifers shift for various reasons. One thing that is known to change underground water flow is road construction during which the blasting of rock is required. There are entire geographic areas in which heavy blasting resulted in wells failing.

Shallow wells depend on specific aquifers in many cases. If the aquifer changes direction and no longer passes within range of the well, the well will dry up. Because of their shallow nature, these wells are susceptible to many potential failure possibilities.

DRILLED WELLS

Drilled wells are more expensive to install than shallow wells, but they are far more dependable. Well drillers can drill through solid bedrock when creating a drilled well. Depths for these wells vary, but most are at least 125 feet deep. My personal well is a little over 300 feet deep, and there are some that are far deeper. An average depth would probably be somewhere in the range of 200 to 250 feet.

The diameter of the casing for a drilled well is normally about 6 inches. This steel casing extends a little above ground level and is covered with a steel cap. The depth to which the casing is installed varies. Essentially, steel casing is installed until the well is encased with bedrock. Grouting is pumped in around the casing to seal the annular space where the casing meets bedrock. This type of construction provides very good protection from well contamination.

Because of the depths of drilled wells, they are rarely affected by dry weather conditions. Shallow wells use a large diameter to store water. Drilled wells use a tall column of water to maintain a suitable water reserve. Both methods work, but drilled wells are the most dependable type of well used for habitable structures.

DRIVEN WELLS

Driven wells, also known as *well points,* are not widely used. They are unreliable and subject to water contamination. People do use driven wells, however, to obtain potable water. Personally, I would not trust the water taken from a well point.

Driven wells are simple in structure. A well point is installed on a drive pipe, which is then driven into the earth. Sections of piping are added as the point is driven deeper. The well point is equipped with a strainer through which water is drawn.

There are many problems associated with well points. The only water available from them is the water that surrounds the point. There is no well system holding a water reserve. Sand can clog the strainer on a well point and render it essentially useless. Depth is another factor. It is not uncommon for well points to stop at a depth of around 20 feet. Others never reach this depth. All in all, I do not consider well points a suitable solution for obtaining potable water.

JETTED WELLS

Jetted wells are not often talked about. The diameters of these wells can range from 2 to 12 inches. Particular soil conditions might prohibit the use of a jetted well. For example, jetted wells cannot be installed in bedrock, limestone, or sandstone. Even boulders and large, loose gravel can prevent the installation of a jetted well. When the soil contains clay, sand, or silt, a jetted well can be used. In 30 years of plumbing I have never seen a jetted well.

ALTERNATIVE WATER SOURCES

Not every home or building is supplied with water from a municipal pipeline or well. Some people get their drinking water from springs. Others obtain water from lakes and cisterns. None of these options are ideal, and contamination is a serious risk with any of these water sources. Although they work fine for irrigation or watering livestock, they are not good choices for potable water. Of the three, springs are generally the best option.

RECOVERY RATE

The recovery rate of any water source must be known in order to size a plumbing system appropriately for the situation. A plumber can determine the minimum daily usage for a plumbing system. A plumber must also size a plumbing system based on the minimum flow rate and the quantity of water required for various types of plumbing fixtures. This is done using tables and information found in the local plumbing code. Table 1.1 is an example of such a table.

The two types of wells used most often are drilled wells and bored wells. A bored well uses a large diameter to store water. Drilled wells use

Table 1.1: Flow Rates and Quantity of Water Required

Plumbing Fixture or Fitting	Maximum Flow Rate or Quantity
Private lavatory	2.2 gpm at 60 psi
Public lavatory	0.25 gal per metering cycle
Public lavatory (unmetered)	0.5 gpm at 60 psi
Showerhead	2.5 gpm at 80 psi
Sink faucet	2.2 gpm at 60 psi
Urinal	1 gal per flushing cycle
Water closet	1.6 gal per flushing cycle

a deep column of water as a water reserve. Both types of wells rely on their recovery rates to keep up with the demands of the plumbing system they serve.

Plumbing systems are sized based on maximum peak demands. For example, a single-family home is assigned a certain demand quantity, while a commercial building has a very different demand factor. The same could be said for a farm application, where the peak demand is based on the number and type of livestock using water.

For a residential scenario, the minimum recovery rate would likely be no less than 3 gallons per minute, and 6 gallons a minute or more is preferable. In simple terms this means that as reserve water in a well is used, the well can replenish it at the prescribed rate.

The sizing of a pump depends on the recovery rate of the well it serves. For example, a pump that delivers water at a rate of 8 gallons a minute would not be a suitable installation for a well that has a recovery rate of 5 gallons per minute. Under constant demand, the pump would drain the well faster than the water reserve could be replaced.

WATER STORAGE TANKS

Some wells have low recovery rates. One way to work around this is to install a large water storage tank. Consider this example: You have a shallow well that recovers 2 gallons per minute, which is a low rate and could cause problems when several plumbing outlets are being used simultaneously. Assume that the well described serves a large family in a home with three bathrooms, and that the family members all shower at approximately the same time each morning. The showerheads being used have a flow rate of 3 gallons per minute. With three showers running at the same time, the result is a flow rate of 9 gallons per minute. The well recovers at a rate of only 2 gallons per minute.

Say that each person spends five minutes in each shower. That is 15 minutes at 9 gallons per minute. Now factor in that the automatic dishwasher and the automatic clothes washer are being used in close conjunction with this timing. It doesn't take long for such usage to put an overwhelming demand on the well.

If there is adequate water reserve in the well, a problem will not be noticed. Once the people leave home for work and school, the well recovers over the course of the day. But apply this same reasoning to a situation where the usage is more constant for a sustained period of time. It would not take long to put a serious strain on the well if the water reserve was not substantial.

One way of getting around this is to install large, aboveground water storage tanks. The tanks provide the first water used when water is demanded at a plumbing outlet. As the reserve in the tank is depleted, the well pump cuts on and refills it. This provides a buffer against draining the well. As soon as the water demand ceases, the well can replenish its water reserve and everything functions normally. This extreme solution is rarely needed or used, but it is an option for situations where the well's rate of recovery is simply not adequate.

2

TYPES OF WELL PUMPS

When working with potable water supplies there are four main types of pumps that you may encounter:

- Submersible pumps
- Shallow-well jet pumps
- Deepwater jet pumps
- Booster pumps

The type of pump selected is often determined by the type of well used to obtain water.

BOOSTER PUMPS

Booster pumps are used in conjunction with other pumps when additional water pressure is required. A booster pump is not a primary well pump. We will discuss these pumps in Chapter 3, as we explore the requirements for pump sizing and meeting flow demands. This chapter concentrates on the three main types of primary well pumps and the basics of when to use them.

SIMPLE PUMP CHOICES

There are some simple pump choices to consider. We will examine the more technical elements of pump selection in Chapter 3. For now, let's look at some of the obvious pros and cons, along with some restrictions that may apply.

Assume that you are working with a bored well that has a depth of 38 feet. You need to lift water approximately 30 feet to meet the demands of the plumbing design. Which type of pump would you use?

In this situation you could install a submersible pump, a one-pipe jet pump, or a two-pipe jet pump. The lift requirement on the pump is low enough that any of these pumps will get the job done.

Now consider a situation where you have a drilled well with a depth of 75 feet. Which types of pumps can be used to deliver water from this well? A shallow-well jet pump will not work. It is not capable of lifting water from such a depth. You can use a deep-well jet pump with a two-pipe system or you can install a submersible pump. In most cases the sensible choice will be a submersible pump.

SHALLOW-WELL JET PUMPS

Shallow-well jet pumps are limited in their abilities. These pumps work on a suction basis. When water is at sea level a shallow-water jet pump can lift it a maximum of just under 34 feet under ideal conditions. Since conditions are rarely ideal, it is a good idea to factor in some loss in water lift. For example, I would not expect a shallow-well jet pump to lift water more than about 30 feet. Pump manufacturers generally suggest that a maximum amount of lift should be figured at 25 feet and that you should deduct 1 foot of lift for every 1000 feet of elevation above sea level. Chapter 3 provides more of this type of information in discussions on pump selection and sizing.

DEEP-WELL JET PUMPS

Deep-well jet pumps rely on a two-pipe system in the well casing. The pump pushes pressure down one pipe to bring it up the other pipe. This arrangement is suitable for wells that are up to 120 feet deep. However, I recommend limiting this use to a depth of 100 feet.

Deep-well jet pumps are also called *convertible* pumps. This is because they can be used as either one-pipe shallow-well pumps or two-pipe deep-well pumps. The piping arrangement makes the difference. Chapter 9 goes into greater detail about this.

SUBMERSIBLE PUMPS

A submersible pumps is the king of deep wells. This pump is installed in the well casing, near the bottom of the well. The downside is servicing the pump. In order to work on a submersible pump you must first remove it from the well, which means removing the piping and electrical wiring that is connected to the pump. This can be done by hand if you have a strong back, but a mechanical pump pulling machine makes the process far easier and much quicker.

Jet pumps are installed above ground. This makes them easier to access when service is required. But submersible pumps are more efficient when lifting water from deep wells. Unlike deep-well jet pumps, submersible pumps are not restricted to certain depths. They push water up the supply pipe, and as long as the pumps are powerful enough to push water the needed distance, they can be used.

A RULE OF THUMB

As a rule of thumb, you can use a single-pipe jet pump when water has to be lifted 25 to 30 feet. Once that amount of lift is exceeded, a two-pipe jet pump can be used for a depth of 100 to 120 feet. Beyond that, a submersible pump is needed.

COST

The cost of a pump goes up as its pumping power increases. Shallow-well jet pumps are the least expensive option. Deep-well jet pumps are next in line, with submersible pumps being the most expensive design to buy. This is probably the main reason that some people use deep-well jet pumps instead of submersible pumps if the well depth allows for such a choice.

Most plumbers and well installers agree that submersible pumps are better than deep-well jet pumps and should be used in all applications other than shallow wells. But sometimes money is a factor at the time of installation, so it is good to be aware of all of your options.

PUMP
SELECTION

Pump selection is a key element in creating a suitable well system. Some people think they can go to a home improvement store and simply buy a pump that looks good and is priced right. This is the wrong approach. Selecting a pump is serious business. To make a good selection you must take into account many factors, such as friction loss and atmospheric pressure. How much water will the pump have to produce to supply the amount of water that will be needed at any given time? What is the recovery rate of the well that the pump will serve? How much lift is going to be required of the pump? There is a lot of knowledge required to make an appropriate pump selection.

Chapter 2 gave you the easy stuff. This chapter gets technical in order to give you the data you need to select and size pumps properly. Here you will find the detailed information required to make important decisions once you know what type of pump you want to use.

REFRESHER COURSE

Here is a short refresher course on the preceding chapter.

Shallow-well jet pumps: These pumps should not be used in cases where water must be lifted in excess of 30 feet. A safer estimation of the height to which a simple jet pump can lift water is 25 feet. These are the least expensive pumps available, but they are very limited because of their maximum lift capability.

Deep-well jet pumps: Deep-well jet pumps can be used to pump water from a depth of up to 120 feet, although I recommend limiting the maximum lift to 100 feet. The price of these pumps falls somewhere between those of shallow-well jet pumps and those of submersible pumps. When cost is a factor, a deep-well jet pump can be the answer, but a submersible pump is preferable in most conditions.

Submersible pumps: Submersible pumps are generally considered to be the cream of the crop. They are the most expensive type of pump normally used in potable water systems. Submersible pumps can lift water from great depths. This makes them the perfect choice for deep wells.

Now you are up to speed and ready to tackle the technical steps involved in choosing and sizing a suitable pump. In fact, Chapter 2 gave you a pretty good handle on how to choose a pump, but this chapter fills in the details to help you make sensible decisions.

FRICTION LOSS

Friction loss is a factor that can come into play when sizing a pump. The type of pipe and fittings connected to the pump affect the amount of friction loss. Most pump installers and plumbers oversize pumps sufficiently to compensate for friction loss without doing a lot of math to determine a base minimum for the required pump size.

An understanding of the effect of friction loss is essential. See Tables 3.1 through 3.3.

Table 3.1 Friction Loss in Schedule-40 Plastic Pipe (in feet of head per 100 ft.)

		3/8"	1/2"	3/4"	1"
GPM	**GPH**	ft.	ft.	ft.	ft.
1	60	4.25	1.38	.356	.11
2	120	15.13	4.83	1.21	.38
3	180	31.97	9.96	2.51	.77
4	240	54.97	17.07	4.21	1.30
5	300	84.41	25.76	6.33	1.92

GPM	GPH	3/8″ ft.	1/2″ ft.	3/4″ ft.	1″ ft.
6	360		36.34	8.83	2.69
8	480		63.71	15.18	4.58
10	600		97.52	25.98	6.88
15	900			49.68	14.67
20	1,200			86.94	25.07
25	1,500				38.41
30	1,800				
35	2,100				
40	2,400				
45	2,700				
50	3,000				
60	3,600				
70	4,200				
80	4,800				
90	5,400				
100	6,000				

(Courtesy of Goulds Pumps)

Table 3.2 Friction Loss in Steel Pipe (in feet of head per 100 ft.)

GPM	GPH	3/8″ ft.	1/2″ ft.	3/4″ ft.	1″ ft.
1	60	4.30	1.86	.26	
2	120	15.00	4.78	1.21	.38
3	180	31.80	10.00	2.50	.77
4	240	54.90	17.10	4.21	1.30
5	300	83.50	25.80	6.32	1.93
6	360		36.50	8.87	2.68
7	420		48.70	11.80	3.56
8	480		62.70	15.00	4.54
10	600			23.00	6.86
12	720			32.60	9.62

(Continued)

Table 3.2 *(Continued)*

GPM	GPH	3⁄8″ ft.	1⁄2″ ft.	3⁄4″ ft.	1″ ft.
15	900			49.70	14.70
20	1,200			86.10	25.10
25	1,500				38.60
30	1,800				54.60
35	2,100				73.40
40	2,400				95.00
45	2,700				
70	4,200				
100	6,000				

(Courtesy of Goulds Pumps)

Table 3.3 Friction Loss in Copper Pipe (in feet of head per 100 ft.)

GPM	GPH	3⁄8″ ft.	1⁄2″ ft.	3⁄4″ ft.	1″ ft.
1	60	6.2	1.8	.39	
2	120	19.6	6.0	1.2	
5	300		30.0	5.8	1.6
7	420		53.0	11.0	3.2
10	600			19.6	5.3
15	900			37.0	9.9
18	1,080			55.4	16.1
20	1,200				18.5
25	1,500				27.7
30	1,800				39.3
35	2,100				48.5
40	2,400				
45	2,700				
50	3,000				
60	3,600				

GPM	GPH	3⁄8″ ft.	1⁄2″ ft.	3⁄4″ ft.	1″ ft.
70	4,200				
75	4,500				
80	4,800				
90	5,400				
100	6,000				

(Courtesy of Goulds Pumps)

Fittings used in a piping assembly account for friction loss. Table 3.4 shows how various fittings affect friction loss. Table 3.5 demonstrates friction loss when a jet pump is offset horizontally from a well.

MINIMUM WATER REQUIREMENTS

Before you can size a water pump you must know the minimum water requirements for the proposed usage. The local plumbing codebook contains plenty of tables and information that can be used for this purpose. Whether you are sizing a pump for a farm, a home, or some other application, you can find minimum requirements in the local plumbing code. Tables 3.6 through 3.10 are representative of the types of tables local codes use to determine minimum plumbing requirements.

HOW DEEP IS THE WATER IN THE WELL?

How deep is the water in the well that you are sizing a pump for? We have talked about depth limitations for jet pumps. It is logical that you will need to know how far into the well your piping will need to be installed.

What method will you use to determine the water depth in the well? There is a technical method for this. See Figure 3.1 for instructions on using a professional technique to determine water depth.

Table 3.4 Friction Loss for Pipe Fittings

Size of fitting, Inches	1/2"	3/4"	1"	1 1/4"	1 1/2"	2"
90° Ell	1.5	2.0	2.7	3.5	4.3	5.5
45° Ell	0.8	1.0	1.3	1.7	2.0	2.5
Long Sweep Ell	1.0	1.4	1.7	2.3	2.7	3.5
Close Return Bend	3.6	5.0	6.0	8.3	10.0	13.0
Tee-Straight Run	1	2	2	3	3	4
Tee-Side Inlet or Outlet or Pitless Adapter	3.3	4.5	5.7	7.6	9.0	12.0
① Ball or Globe Valve Open	17.0	22.0	27.0	36.0	43.0	55.0
① Angle Valve Open	8.4	12.0	15.0	18.0	22.0	28.0
Gate Valve-Fully Open	0.4	0.5	0.6	0.8	1.0	1.2
Check Valve (Swing)	4	5	7	9	11	13
In Line Check Valve (Spring) or Foot Valve	4	6	8	12	14	19

① There are many new, full port valve designs available today which are more efficient and create much less friction loss, consult with valve suppliers for new data.

Example:

(A) 100 ft. of 2" plastic pipe with one (1) 90° elbow.(B) Assume flow to be 80 GPM through 2" plastic pipe. and one (1) swing check valve.

90° elbow – equivalent to   5.5 ft. of straight pipe
Swing check-equivalentto   13.0 ft. of straight pipe
100 ft. of pipe – equivalent to 100 ft. of straight pipe
                118.5 ft. = Total
                equivalent pipe

1. Friction loss table shows 11.43 ft. loss per 100 ft. of pipe.

2. In step (A) above we have determined total ft. of pipe to be 118.5 ft.

3. Convert 118.5 ft. to percentage 118.5 ÷ 100 = 1.185

4. Multiply   11.43
        ×1.185
    13.54455 or 13.5 ft. = Total friction loss in this system.

Figure friction loss for 118.5 ft. of pipe.
(Courtesy of Goulds Pumps)

Table 3.5 Offset Jet Pump Pipe Friction (Friction Loss in Feet Per 100 Feet Offset)

Jet Size Hp	Suction And Pressure Pipe Sizes (In inches)			
	$1\frac{1}{4} \times 1$	$1\frac{1}{4} \times 1\frac{1}{4}$	$1\frac{1}{2} \times 1\frac{1}{4}$	$1\frac{1}{2} \times 1\frac{1}{2}$
1/3	12	8	6	4
1/2	18	12	8	6
3/4		22	16	11
1			25	16
1½			Operations Below Line Not Recommended	
2				
3				

NOTE: Friction loss is to be added to vertical lift.

(Courtesy of Goulds Pumps)

Table 3.6 Water Rates for Private Residences

Outlets	Flow Rate GPM	Total Usage Gallons	Bathrooms in Home			
			1	1½	2-2½	3-4
Shower or Bathtub	5	35	35	35	53	70
Lavatory	4	2	2	4	6	8
Toilet	4	5	5	10	15	20
Kitchen Sink	5	3	3	3	3	3
Automatic Washer	5	35	-	18	18	18
Dishwasher	2	14	-	-	3	3
Normal seven minute* peak demand (gallons)			45	70	98	122

(Continued)

Table 3.6 (Continued)

Outlets	Flow Rate GPM	Total Usage Gallons	Bathrooms in Home			
			1	1½	2-2½	3-4
Minimum sized pump required to meet peak demand without supplemental supply			7 GPM(420 GPH)	10 GPM(600 GPH)	14 GPM(840 GPH)	17 GPM(1020 GPH)

Notes: Values given are average and do not include higher or lower extremes.

* Peak demand can occur several times during morning and evening hours.

** Count the number of fixtures in a home including outside hose bibs. Supply one gallon per minute each.

(Courtesy of Goulds Pumps)

Table 3.7 Flow Rates for Common Yard Fixtures

Garden Hose – ½ "	3 GPM
Garden Hose – ¾ "	6 GPM
Sprinkler – Lawn	3-7 GPM

(Courtesy of Goulds Pumps)

Table 3.8 Water Requirements for Farm Usage

Horse, Steer	12 Gallons per day
Dry Cow	15 Gallons per day
Milking Cow	35 Gallons per day
Hog	4 Gallons per day
Sheep	2 Gallons per day
Chickens/100	6 Gallons per day
Turkeys/100	20 Gallons per day
Fire	20-60 GPM

(Courtesy of Goulds Pumps)

Table 3.9 Pump Capacity Required for Public Buildings

	Pump Capacity Required in U.S. Gallons per Minute per fixture for Public Buildings						
	Total Number of Fixtures						
Type of Building	**25 or Less**	**26-50**	**51-100**	**101-200**	**201-400**	**401-600**	**Over 600**
Hospitals	1.00	1.00	.80	.60	.50	.45	.40
Mercantile Buildings	1.30	1.00	.80	.71	.60	.54	.48
Office Buildings	1.20	.90	.72	.65	.50	.40	.35
Schools	1.20	.85	.65	.60	.55	.45	
Hotels, Motels	.80	.60	.55	.45	.40	.35	.33
Apartment Buildings	.60	.50	.37	.30	.28	.25	.24

[1]For less than 25 fixtures, pump capacity should not be less than 75% of capacity required for 25 fixtures.

[2]Where additional water is required for some special process, this should be added to pump capacity.

[3]Where laundries or swimming pools are to be supplied, add approximately 10% to pump capacity for either.

[4]Where the majority of occupants are women, add approximately 20% to pump capacity.

(Courtesy of Goulds Pumps)

Table 3.10 Boiler Feed Requirements

Boiler		Boiler		Boiler		Boiler		Boiler	
HP	**GPM**	**HP**	**GPM**	**HP**	**GPM**	**HP**	**GPM**	**HP**	**GPM**
20	1.38	55	3.80	90	6.21	160	11.1	275	19.0
25	1.73	60	4.14	100	6.90	170	11.7	300	20.7
30	2.07	65	4.49	110	7.59	180	12.4	325	22.5
35	2.42	70	4.83	120	8.29	190	13.1	350	24.2
40	2.76	75	5.18	130	8.97	200	13.8	400	27.6

(Continued)

Table 3.10 *(Continued)*

Boiler		Boiler		Boiler		Boiler		Boiler	
HP	GPM	HP	GPM	HP	GPM	HP	GPM	HP	GPM
45	3.11	80	5.52	140	9.66	225	15.5	450	31.1
50	3.45	85	5.87	150	10.4	250	17.3	500	34.5

[1]Boiler Horsepower equals 34.5 lb. water evaporated at and from 212°F, and requires feed water at a rate of 0.069 gpm.

Select the boiler feed pump with a capacity of 2 to 3 times greater than the figures given above at a pressure 20 to 25% above that of boiler, because the table gives equivalents of boiler horsepower without reference to fluctuating demands.

(Courtesy of Goulds Pumps)

Determining Water Level

Install ⅛″ or ¼″ tubing long enough to be 10′ to 15′ below low water level. Measure the tubing length as it is lowered into the well.

Once the tubing is fixed in a stationary position at the top, connect an air line and pressure gauge. Add air to the tubing until the pressure gauge reaches a point that it doesn't read any higher. Take a gauge reading at this point.

A. *Depth to water (to be determined).*
B. *Total length of air line (in feet).*
C. *Water pressure on air tubing. Gauge reads in pounds. Convert to feet by multiplying by 2.31.*

Example:

If the air tube is 100′ long, and the gauge reads 20 lbs.
20 lbs. × 2.31 = 46.2 ft.
Length of tube = 100 ft.
minus 46.2 ft. = 53.8 ft.
Depth to water (A) would be 53.8 ft.

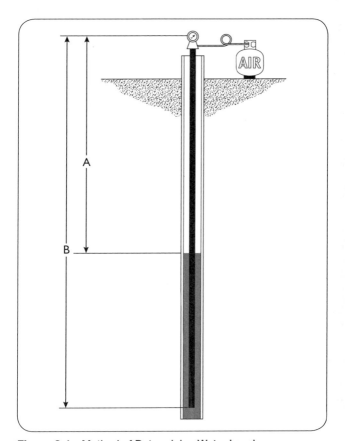

Figure 3.1 Method of Determining Water Level
(Courtesy of Goulds Pumps)

The procedure described in Figure 3.1 is a detailed, accurate way of determining the water level in a well. I admit that I have never used it. Plumbers in the field often resort to other methods.

When I am preparing to hang a pump or foot valve in a well I want to know the total depth of the well. This information is usually readily available from the well installer. It is common for well drillers to provide information on the total well depth and the recovery rate of the well. However, they may not provide details on how deep the water in the well is.

Determining water depth in a shallow well is easy. Glue two 20-foot sections of rigid plastic piping together and push this pipe into the water and to the bottom of the well. Since most shallow wells are less than 40 feet deep, there should be pipe showing above the water level. You can simply measure the distance between the water level and the top of the pipe that is above the water. If there is 6 feet of pipe sticking out of the water, the depth of the water in the well is 34 feet. This method is easy, since the well diameter is large and allows plenty of visibility and limited depth. The situation changes for deep wells.

Assume that you are working with a drilled well that is 225 feet deep. How do you determine where the static head of water terminates in the well casing? If you remove the well cap you may be able to see the water. It is not uncommon for a drilled well to be somewhat of an artesian well. I have even seen instances where the well water ran over the lip of the well casing. This is not always the case, however.

A visual inspection down the well casing may not reveal the water level. In this situation I use a flat washer and some jute twine to determine the water depth. This is how to proceed.

The first step is to be sure that you have enough twine on a spool to reach the bottom of the well. Tie a heavy, flat washer securely to the loose end of the twine. Now you have two options. The first one is faster, when it works.

Lower the weighted twine into the casing slowly. Listen carefully for any slight splashing sound that might occur when the washer enters the water. You may not be able to hear it, but an experienced plumber can often feel a difference in the handling of the twine once it is passing through water. If you don't have the touch ability and you don't hear anything, lower 25 feet of twine into the well casing. Let it stand for a couple of minutes, which allows it to absorb water if the twine is immersed.

Retrieve the twine and inspect it to see whether any of it is wet. If the line is dry, lower it to a depth of 50 feet and repeat the process. Once the twine has been in the water you will be able to see it upon visual inspection.

For the sake of this example, let's say that you hit water after lowering 25 feet of twine into the well. When you examine the twine you see that the first 5 feet of it measuring from the flat washer is wet and the rest is dry. This means that the static head of the water is located about 20 feet below the lip of the well casing. Thus, there is approximately 205 feet of water in the well.

My personal method for establishing water depth is not very scientific. Neither is it technical. But it does work very well. Regardless of the method you choose to use, you do need to confirm the depth of water in a well before installing a submersible pump or foot valve for a deep-well jet pump.

RECOVERY RATE

Chapter 1 briefly discussed the recovery rate of wells. This rate has a lot to do with the size of the pump that needs to be installed for a given application. The key is to avoid installing a pump that is so powerful that it is capable of pumping the well dry. Obtain recovery rate information from the well installer or the general contractor to help you decide what is needed from the pump you ultimately select.

Some wells have weak recovery rates, which is problematic. In the case of a deep well that is equipped with an assembly for a jet pump there is a way to help offset the slow recovery rate. Although it does not correct the problem, it is a technique for dealing with it.

Normally a foot valve is attached to the jet assembly of a two-pipe well system. If you are working with a well that has a slow recovery rate, the pump may draw down the water level to a point where air is sucked into the foot valve. If this happens, the pump will not produce water as it should. The simple solution for this problem is to install a section of piping between the jet assembly and the foot valve to extend the foot valve to a deeper point in the well water. Figure 3.2 illustrates this procedure and the potential lengths of the section of piping that you are adding, which is referred to in the field as a *tail pipe*.

Tail Pipe

HOW TO USE TAIL PIPE ON DEEP WELL JET PUMPS

Pipe below the jet, or "tail pipe" as it is commonly known, is used when you have a weak deep well. Under normal conditions, the jet assembly with the foot valve attached is lowered into the well. You receive your rated capacity at the level you locate the jet assembly. On a weak well, as the water level lowers to the level of the foot valve (attached to the bottom of the jet assembly), air enters the system. By adding 34' of tail pipe below the jet assembly with the foot valve attached to the bottom of the 34' length of pipe, it will not be possible to pull the well down and allow air to enter the system. The drawing indicates the approximate percentage of rated capacity you will receive with tail pipe.

Using a tail pipe, the pump delivery remains at 100% at sea level of the rated capacity down to the jet assembly level. If water level falls below that, flow decreases in proportion to drawdown as shown in the illustration. When pump delivery equals well inflow, the water level remains constant until the pump shuts off.

This rule can also be used when determining suction pipe length on shallow well systems.

(Courtesy of Goulds Pumps)

You can use flow rates, conversion tables, equations, and a host of other elements to determine the desired minimum water capacity that will be available from a pump. This is all well and good, but it doesn't matter much if the well that you are working with does not have an adequate recovery rate and storage capacity to keep the water flowing. It may be necessary to utilize more than one well to meet the needs of a plumbing system. Water storage tanks may be required. It all starts with the storage capacity and recovery rate of the well in question. (Refer to Figure 3.3 and Tables 3.11 and 3.12.)

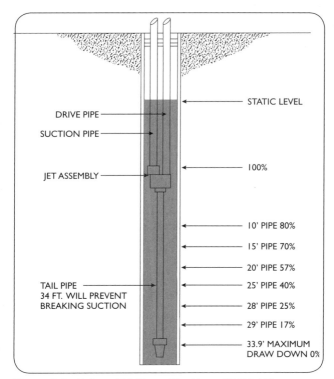

Figure 3.2 Using a Tail Pipe with a Deep-Well Jet Pump
(Courtesy of Goulds Pumps)

WATER PRESSURE

Water pressure is another consideration when sizing a pump. A residential dwelling should be provided with a minimum of 40 pounds per square inch (psi). A pressure rating of 50 to 60 psi is better. This part of a sizing

PIPE NOT RUNNING FULL – CALCULATION OF
DISCHARGE RATE USING AREA FACTOR METHOD

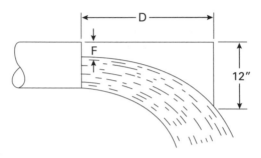

Flow From Horizontal Pipe (not full)

Flow (GPM) = A × D × 1.093 × F

A = Area of pipe in square inches
D = Horizontal distance in inches
F = Effective area factor from chart
Area of pipe equals inside Dia.^{2} × 0.7854
Example: Pipe inside diameter = 10 in.
D = 20 in.
F = 2½ in.
A = 10 × 10 × 0.7854 = 78.54 square in.
F = 0.805
Flow = 78.54 × 20 × 1.039 × 0.805 = 1314 GPM

Figure 3.3 Determining Flow Rates

Ratio F/D = R%	Eff. Area Factor F	Ratio F/D = R%	Eff. Area Factor F
5	0.981	55	0.436
10	0.948	60	0.373
15	0.905	65	0.312
20	0.858	70	0.253
25	0.805	75	0.195
30	0.747	80	0.142
35	0.688	85	0.095
40	0.627	90	0.052
45	0.564	95	0.019
50	0.500	100	0.000

DISCHARGE RATE IN GALLONS PER MINUTE/NOMINAL PIPE SIZE (ID)

Horizontal Dist. (A) Inches	1″	1¼″	1½″	2″
4	5.7	9.8	13.3	22.0
5	7.1	12.2	16.6	27.5
6	8.5	14.7	20.0	33.0
7	10.0	17.1	23.2	38.5
8	11.3	19.6	26.5	44.0
9	12.8	22.0	29.8	49.5
10	14.2	24.5	33.2	55.5
11	15.6	27.0	36.5	60.5
12	17.0	29.0	40.0	66.0
13	18.5	31.5	43.0	71.5
14	20.0	34.0	46.5	77.0
15	21.3	36.3	50.0	82.5
16	22.7	39.0	53.0	88.0
17		41.5	56.5	93.0
18			60.0	99.0
19				110

(Continued)

Horizontal Dist. (A) Inches	1"	1¼"	1½"	2"
20				
21				
22				

(Courtesy of Goulds Pumps)

Table 3.11 Storage of Water in Various Size Pipes
Pipe Volume and Velocity
STORAGE OF WATER IN VARIOUS SIZE PIPES

Pipe Size	Volume in Gallons per Foot	Pipe Size	Volume in Gallons per Foot
1¼	.06	6	1.4
1½	.09	8	2.6
2	.16	10	4.07
3	.36	12	5.87
4	.652		

(Courtesy of Goulds Pumps)

Table 3.12 Storage of Water in Various Sizes of Wells

$$\frac{D^2}{24.5} = \text{Gals. of Storage per Foot}$$

Where: D = Inside diameter of well casing in inches
Examples:

2" Casing = .16 Gals. per ft. Storage	8" Casing = 2.6 Gals. per ft. Storage
3" Casing = .36 Gals. per ft. Storage	10" Casing = 4.07 Gals. per ft. Storage
4" Casing = .652 Gals. per ft. Storage	12" Casing = 5.87 Gals. per ft. Storage
5" Casing = 1.02 Gals. per ft. Storage	14" Casing = 7.99 Gals. per ft. Storage
6" Casing = 1.4 Gals. per ft. Storage	16" Casing = 10.44 Gals. per ft. Storage

(Courtesy of Goulds Pumps)

design has more to do with pressure tanks and pressure switches. However, the pump being used must be capable of filling the pressure tank quickly enough to maintain good water pressure.

PLANNING FOR FUTURE USE CONDITIONS

It is wise to plan for future use conditions when sizing a pump. If you size a pump to meet the minimum demands of the known plumbing system you could be disappointed later in the life of the system. Suppose the property owner wants to expand the plumbing system. If the pump is not large enough, it will not be able to handle the changes. For this reason it makes sense to slightly oversize a pump in consideration of potential upgrades of the plumbing system.

SUMMARY

There are a number of factors that come into play when you are selecting and sizing a pump. Table 3.13 pulls it all together into a basic checklist of items to consider.

Table 3.13 Checklist of Considerations When Selecting and Sizing a Water Pump

Condition	Checked
Type of pump to install	
Friction loss	
Minimum water requirements	
Water depth in well	
Well recovery rate	
Gallons per minute that pump is capable of supplying	
Cost of the pump	
Potential future use additional needs	

(Continued)

Table 3.13 *(Continued)*

Condition	Checked
Cost of labor to install the pump system	
Cost of material to install the pump system	
Available electrical power supply ratings	
Pump reliability and warranty	
Pump maintenance and service cost factors	
Operating expense of the pump	
Availability of the pump	

You can use the plumbing code and recommendations from pump manufacturers to aid you in your selection and sizing tasks. Those materials, along with the information in this chapter, should prepare you to make wise decisions. Take the time to do this part of your job correctly. If you select and install a pump that is inappropriate for the system it serves, the financial pain can be substantial and your reputation might be called into question.

4

WELL PRESSURE TANKS

How much do you know about well pressure tanks? I have been a master plumber for more than 30 years. During those years I have worked with a lot of plumbers, well drillers, and well pump installers. It has always surprised me how little some of these professionals know about pressure tanks. A lot of the pros pay scant attention to the pressure tanks. They know they are needed and they know how to install them, but it is a shame how many of them do not understand the importance of proper sizing considerations.

Pressure tanks are essential to the proper operation of a well system. There are four basic types of tanks in common use to choose from:

- In-line models (see Figure 4.1)
- Stand models (see Figure 4.2)
- Underground models (see Figure 4.3)
- Pump stand models (see Figure 4.4)

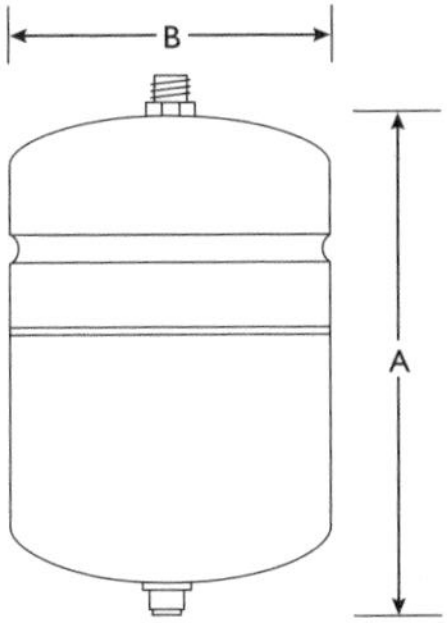

In-Line Models

Model No.	Tank Vol.		Max. Accept. Factor	A Height		B Diameter		Sys. Conn.[1]	Factory Pre-charge	Working Pressure[2]
	Lit.	Gal		mm	ins.	mm	ins.	ins.	PSIG	PSIG
WX-101	8	2.0	0.45	321	12⅝	203	8	¾	18	100
WX-102	17	4.4	0.55	381	15	279	11	¾	18	100
WX-103	33	7.6	0.42	629	22¼	279	11	¾	28	100
WX-104	39	10.3	1.00	451	17¾	390	15⅜	1	38	125
WX-200	53	14.0	0.81	559	22	390	15⅜	1	38	125

System Connection: Stainless Steel Waterway.

[1] System Connection: Stainless Steel Waterway.
[2] 100 PSIG is 689.5 kPa, 125 PSIG is 862 kPa

Figure 4.1 In-Line Models
(Courtesy of Amtrol, Inc.)

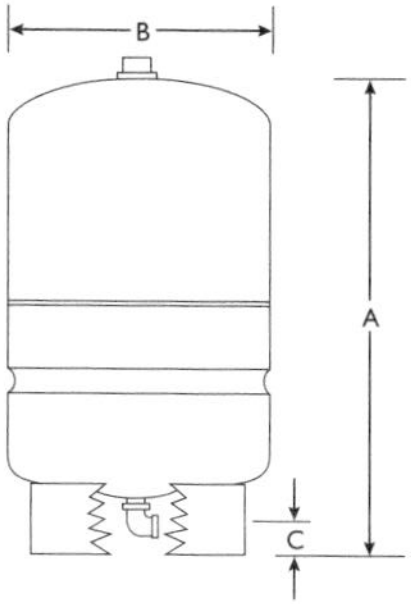

Stand Models

Model No.	Tank vol.		Max. Accept. Factor	A Height		B Diameter		C Conn.	Sys. Conn.[3]	Factory Pre-charge	Working Pressure
	Lit.	Gal		mm	ins.	mm	ins.	ins.	ins.	PSIG	PSIG[2]
WX-104-S	39	10.3	1.00	489	19 1/4	390	15 3/8	1 13/16	1	38	125
WX-201	53	14.0	0.81	606	23 7/8	390	15 3/8	1 13/16	1	38	125
WX-202	76	20.0	0.57	803	31 5/8	390	15 3/8	1 13/16	1	38	125
WX-202XL	98.4	26.0	0.44	971.5	38 1/4	390.5	15 3/8	1 13/16	1	38	125
WX-203	121	32.0	0.35	1143	45	390	15 3/8	1 13/16	1	38	125
WX-205	129	34.0	1.00	752	29 5/8	559	22	2 3/16	1 1/4	38	125
WX-250	167	44.0	0.77	914	36	559	22	2 3/16	1 1/4	38	125
WX-251	235	62.0	0.55	1187	46 3/4	559	22	2 3/16	1 1/4	38	125
WX-255	306.6	81.0	0.41	1432	56 3/8	558.8	22	2 3/16	1 1/4	38	125
WX-302	326	86.0	0.54	1200	47 1/4	660	26	2 3/16	1 1/4	38	125
WX-350	450	119.0	0.39	1572	61 7/8	660	26	2 3/16	1 1/4	38	125

[2] 125 PSIG is 862 kPa

[3] System Connection: Stainless Steel.

Figure 4.2 Stand Models

(Courtesy of Amtrol, Inc.)

| Model No. | Tank Vol. | | Max. Accept. Factor | Height | | Diameter | | Sys. Conn.[1] ins. | Factory Precharge PSIG |
	Lit.	Gal		mm	ins.	mm	ins.		
WX-200-UG	53	14.0	0.81	559	22	390	15⅜	1	38
WX-202-UG	76	20.0	0.57	726	30	390	15⅜	1	38
WX-250-UG	167	44.0	0.77	848	33⅜	559	22	1¼	38
WX-251-UG	235	62.0	0.55	1121	44⅛	559	22	1¼	38

Underground Models

[1] System Connection: Stainless Steel Coupling.
Coating on underground models is an epoxy-based paint.
Working Pressure: 125 PSIG (862 kPa)

Figure 4.3 Underground Models
(Courtesy of Amtrol, Inc.)

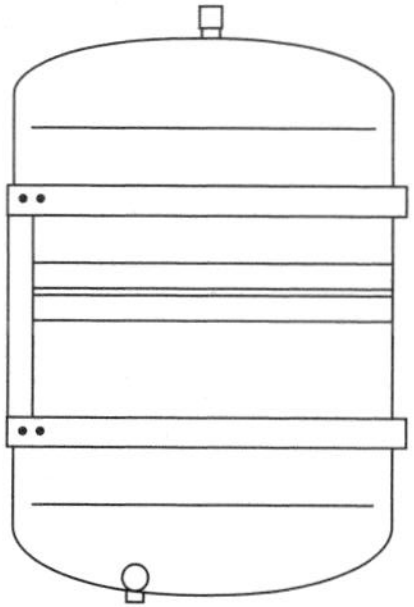

Pump Stand Models

Model No.	Tank Vol. Lit.	Tank Vol. Gal	Max. Accept. Factor	Height mm	Height ins.	Width mm	Width ins.	Length mm	Length ins.	Sys Conn.[1] ins.	Factory Precharge PSIG
WX-102-PS	17	4.4	0.55	318	12½	235	9¼	362	14¼	¾	18
WX-105-PS	20	5.3	0.80	279	11	268	10 9/10	464	18¼	¾	18
WX-200-PS	53	14.0	0.81	407	16	391	15⅜	530	20⅞	1	28

[1] **System Connection:** Stainless Steel Waterway.
Working Pressure: WX-105-PS 100 PSIG (689.5 kPa); WX-200-PS 125 PSIG (862 kPa)

Figure 4.4 Pump Stand Models
(Courtesy of Amtrol, Inc.)

All pressure tanks have maximum operating limitations. This includes the operating temperature and the working pressure. See Table 4.1 for an example of one manufacturer's ratings for maximum operation conditions.

Table 4.1 Maximum Operating Conditions

(Courtesy of Amtrol, Inc.)

Operating Temperature	200° F(93° C)
Working Pressure Model WX-105 PS	100 PSIG (689.5 kPa)
Working Pressure Models WX-200 UG Through WX-251-UG, WX-200-PS	125 PSIG (862 kPa)

Complies with Low Lead Plumbing Law

Modern pressure tanks are built with an internal diaphragm. This device provides a dependable air cushion in the tank. The tanks are shipped with precharged air content. The air provided at the factory is normally installed at a rate of 38 psi, which prevents the tank from becoming waterlogged. A tank that is waterlogged puts excessive demand on a pump that will reduce the pump life. Having a waterlogged pressure tank is nearly as bad as having no pressure tank at all. See Figure 4.5 for technical data on a stand-type pressure tank from a major manufacturer.

Well pressure tanks that are not sized or working properly can shorten the life of a pump. They also deliver lower water pressure, which does not make for happy customers. Must you install a pressure tank for a water pump to supply water to a water distribution system? No, but if you don't, the system will not be acceptable according to professional standards.

Water pumps deliver water volume. They do not deliver much water pressure. A pressure tank installed between the pump and the water distribution system provides the desired water pressure. The pump and the pressure tank must work together to provide optimum service.

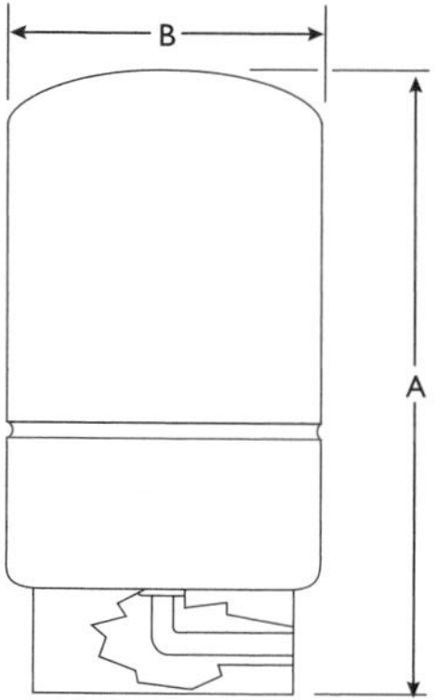

Stand Models

Model No.	Tank Vol. Lit	Tank Vol. Gal	Max. Accept. Factor	A Height mm	A Height ins.	B Diameter mm	B Diameter ins.	Sys. Conn. ins.	Factory Pre-charge PSIG	Working Pressure PSIG[1]
WX-202P	76	20.0	0.57	803	31⅝	390	15⅜	1	38	125
WX-202XLP	98.4	26.0	0.44	971.5	38¼	390.5	15⅜	1	38	125
WX-203P	121	32.0	0.35	1181	46½	390	15⅜	1	38	125
WX-205P	129	34.0	1.00	752	29⅝	559	22	1¼	38	125
WX-250P	167	44.0	0.77	914	36	559	22	1¼	38	125
WX-251P	235	62.0	0.55	1187	46¾	559	22	1¼	38	125
WX-255P	306.6	81.0	0.41	1432	56⅜	558.8	22	1¼	38	125
WX-302P	326	86.0	0.54	1200	47¼	660	26	1¼	38	125
WX-350P	450	119.0	0.39	1572	61⅞	660	26	1¼	38	125

[1] 125 PSIG is 862 kPa.

Figure 4.5 Stand Model Technical Data
(Courtesy of Amtrol, Inc.)

39

STAND MODELS

Stand models are probably the more prevalent type of well pressure tanks used in modern plumbing systems. They range in capacity from about 10 gallons to a little over 100 gallons. The average working pressure for these tanks is 125 psi. So you can choose from within a range of 10 gallons to 100 gallons. How do you make the selection? There are some simple considerations to address first.

Size can be a factor. In some installations there is not enough space available for a large pressure tank. For example, let's look at the dimensions of a 20-gallon tank and those of a 62-gallon tank.

A 20-gallon tank stands about 31 inches tall. The 62-gallon model rises to a height of about 46 inches. If you have only 36 inches of height clearance to work with, the larger tank is out. You should also consider the diameters of the two tanks. The 20-gallon tank has a diameter of about 15 inches, while the 62-gallon tank has a diameter that is close to 22 inches. Again, the amount of available space would affect your choice of tanks. Other considerations will be covered later in this chapter.

Stand models are popular because they are available in a range of sizes and because they support their own weight. Not all pressure tanks do this. As a master plumber, I prefer to use stand models whenever I can, and many installers share my sentiment.

IN-LINE MODELS

In-line pressure tanks have very limited holding capacity. A small model will hold only 2 gallons, and 14 gallons is about the average maximum capacity that you can find. This is not a lot of reserve water, and a pump will cycle more often than it should when the holding capacity is this low.

So why would you use an in-line tank? As the name implies, these tanks are piped right into the water supply and water distribution piping.

They take up very little space and are usually suspended from floor joists. When you have limited space to work with as well as limited demand on the pump, an in-line tank is a viable option. Otherwise, avoid using this type.

PUMP STAND MODELS

Pump stand pressure tanks are used in conjunction with jet pumps. This is true of both shallow-well jet pumps and deep-well jet pumps. The pressure tank sits on the floor and has a mounting bracket built into the top of it. This allows the jet pump to be mounted on the tank to conserve space. However, like the in-line models, capacity ranges for pump stand tanks are very limited. The most you can expect them to hold is around 14 gallons. I recommend using pressure tanks with more capacity, but these tanks are convenient and they do save space.

UNDERGROUND MODELS

Underground pressure tanks have the potential for a large holding capacity. They generally hold up to 62 gallons. Since the tanks are installed below ground, they do not take up any room within a building. This is a plus. However, the fact that they are buried could be an inconvenience when it comes to servicing the system. Underground pressure tanks must be installed in a vertical position, and they must be protected from freezing.

Underground tanks are generally equipped with stainless steel couplings for connecting them to the water service. The tanks are usually coated with an epoxy-based paint. I have more than 30 years of field experience, much of it in rural areas, and I have never encountered an underground pressure tank.

HOW DOES A DIAPHRAGM PRESSURE TANK WORK?

Generally, diaphragm pressure tanks work very well. They are quite dependable. As I mentioned earlier, these tanks come from the factory with an air charge of about 38 psi in them, which means that they are connect-and-go tanks. You do not have to balance them because the manufacturer has already done that for you.

In the old days, pressure tanks were generally just galvanized steel tanks with an air valve installed in the top of them. An installer had to pump air into the tank before filling it with water. Getting the right amount of air for maximum performance could be something of a trial-and-error experience. When the galvanized tanks rusted and leaked, the air escaped. This allowed water to fill most, if not all, of the tank. The result was a waterlogged tank.

When a pressure tank is waterlogged it does not regulate pressure properly. Basically, the pressure delivered to the water distribution system is no more than what the pump is providing, and that is not much. Not only is there a lack of appropriate water pressure, the pump must cut on and run every time water is called for. These starts and stops shorten the working life of the pump. Air has to be reintroduced into a waterlogged tank to return it to working condition. With modern pressure tanks, this is not a concern. They just work. When they don't, it is time to replace them.

The type of well pressure tank that I install holds the water in a molded rigid polypropylene liner supported by an outer steel shell. The diaphragm is installed over the water liner. With this type of design, the water is noncorrosive.

When water is allowed to enter the tank, the water liner expands. The diaphragm acts as a buffer that holds the liner down with the use of air pressure. There is no strain on the diaphragm, since the water pressure and the air pressure are constantly balanced. Water pressure is controlled by a pressure switch, which we will discuss more when we consider installation methods for well pressure tanks. (See Figure 4.6.)

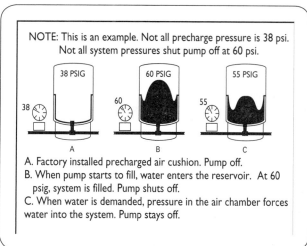

NOTE: This is an example. Not all precharge pressure is 38 psi. Not all system pressures shut pump off at 60 psi.

38 PSIG   60 PSIG   55 PSIG

A   B   C

A. Factory installed precharged air cushion. Pump off.
B. When pump starts to fill, water enters the reservoir. At 60 psig, system is filled. Pump shuts off.
C. When water is demanded, pressure in the air chamber forces water into the system. Pump stays off.

Figure 4.6 Visual Example of Diaphragm Well Pressure Tanks *(Courtesy of Amtrol, Inc.)*

PRESSURE TANK CAPACITY

You will need to determine the capacity that is acceptable for a well pressure tank that you are going to install. Some customers tell the installer the size of the tank they want or are willing to pay for. If your customer is making an inappropriate decision, you should be prepared to explain why a larger pressure tank is recommended.

Your goal in sizing the pressure tank is to choose a tank that will not strain the pump it serves and will give the user of the plumbing system adequate water supply and pressure. You must consider several factors.

Once you know the size of the pump you will be installing, you can begin to determine the size of the pressure tank that will provide quality service. The number of times that a pump should operate during a 24-hour period is based on the horsepower rating of the pump. See Table 4.2 for the recommended numbers of daily starts and stops for pumps of various sizes.

Table 4.2 Suggested Maximum Number of Pump Starts Per Day

Motor Rating	Single-Phase Pump	Three-Phase Pump
Up to 3/4 horsepower (hp)	300	300
1 hp through 5 hp	100	300
7½ hp through 30 hp	50	100

When you know how many daily starts the pump should be expected to deliver without undue strain, you can begin to determine how large the well pressure tank will need to be. To make this assessment, you need to consider the plumbing fixtures that will be connected to the water distribution supply. You will want data on the normal daily water usage requirements, and it is helpful to know the average flow rates for different types of fixtures. See Tables 4.3, 4.4, and 4.5 for examples of this type of information.

After you have determined the estimated volume of water that will be needed in the course of a day, you can analyze it further by anticipating peak times of usage. If you are dealing with a business, the peak usage is likely to be spread out over a period of up to 12 hours a day. There should be minimal usage when the business is closed. For this type of situation you need to prepare for the potential of high usage for several hours at a time and then a long period of time with little usage.

In the case of a home, there will likely be heavy usage for maybe an hour each morning. Then usage normally drops while residents are at work and school. When the occupants return home, usage will goes back up. There is likely to be a spike in late afternoon. Then there may be demands for dishwashing and washing clothes in the evening. Before bed there is normally increased usage, and then the system is at rest during sleeping hours.

Table 4.3 Sample Flow Rate Requirements for Domestic Plumbing Fixtures

Type of Domestic Fixtures	Average Flow Rate (rates given in gallons per minute (GPM) or gallons per hour (GPH)
Toilet	1.5–5 gpm with an average of 3 gpm
Bathtub	3–5 gpm
Shower	3–5 gpm
Lavatory	3 gpm
Kitchen sink	3 gpm
½-in. water hose	200 gph
¾-in. water hose	300 gph
Lawn sprinkler	120 gph

Table 4.4 Sample Water Usage Requirements

Type of Usage	Volume
Per person per day in a home	75 gal.
Taking a shower or bath	Up to 30 gal.
Filling a bathtub	Up to 30 gal.
Flushing a toilet	1.5–5 gal.
Filling a lavatory	2 gal.
Domestic dishwasher per load	7 gal.
Clothes washer per load	Up to 50 gal.

Table 4.5 Conversion Factors for Volume

1 U.S. gallon	231 cubic inches
1 U.S. gallon	3.785 liters
1 Imperial gallon	1.2 U.S. gallons
1 barrel (oil)	42 U.S. gallons
1 cubic foot	7.48 U.S. gallons

Sizing a pressure tank for a home generally means that you have to prepare for periodic high usage with several lulls in between. How much water would a family of four use in 30 minutes? Conversion tables like those provided here can give you a good idea of what to expect.

There is guesswork involved when estimating water usage demands. Ideally, you should err on the side of caution in your estimates and install a pressure tank that is larger than the expectation of what will be needed.

PREINSTALLATION PROCESS

There is a preinstallation process that should be conducted when you prepare to install a well pressure tank. At the start of the installation, take note of the location of the air valve. The tank should have been charged with air before it was made available for sale. A standard factory charge will be about 38 psi, but this may be too much pressure for your installation. It is also possible that the tank lost air pressure before you obtained it. Therefore, you should apply an air gauge to the air valve and confirm the actual air pressure contained in the tank. You should find the charge to be within 10 percent one way or the other of the factory precharge.

Next, you need to adjust the air pressure so that it is within an acceptable range for the pressure switch that you will be installing in the well system. Ideally, the air pressure should be about 2 psi below the cut-in setting that the pressure switch used with the tank will have. In other words, if you are using a 30/50-psi pressure switch, the cut-in pressure is 30 psi and the cut-out pressure is 50 psi. Knowing this, you want the air pressure in the tank to be established at 28 psi. In the case of a 40/60-psi pressure switch, the air pressure would be set at 38 psi. This preinstallation process is an important part of a proper installation.

MOUNTING A PRESSURE TANK

The process of mounting a pressure tank begins with positioning the tank in its operating location. Let's look at each type of pressure tank and how they are likely to be set or mounted.

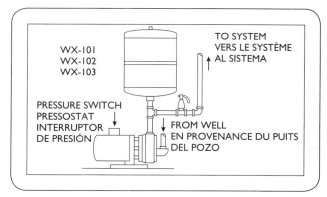

WX-101
WX-102
WX-103

PRESSURE SWITCH
PRESSOSTAT
INTERRUPTOR
DE PRESIÓN

TO SYSTEM
VERS LE SYSTÈME
AL SISTEMA

FROM WELL
EN PROVENANCE DU PUITS
DEL POZO

Figure 4.7 Typical Installation of an In-Line Pressure Tank
(Courtesy of Amtrol, Inc.)

POSITIONING IN-LINE TANKS

There are different methods for positioning in-line pressure tanks. For our example, assume that the tank is being used in conjunction with a jet pump. A common way of installing the tank is to mount it vertically on a steel pipe nipple close to the pump. Figure 4.7 shows an example of this type of positioning.

Another way to install an in-line tank is to position it into the system between two pieces of pipe. This is normally done by placing a tee fitting on its back in horizontal piping. The weight of the tank in this type of installation is supported by pipe hangers that are normally installed in floor joists. The hangers extend downward and go under the piping. Any hangers used must be capable of supporting the full weight of the tank and its contents.

MOUNTING A PUMP STAND MODEL

Mounting a pump stand pressure tank is pretty simple. Find a solid, level surface and place the tank on it. The pump mount is on the top of the tank

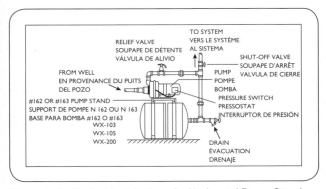

Figure 4.8 Typical Installation of a Horizontal Pump Stand Model Pressure Tank

(Courtesy of Amtrol, Inc.)

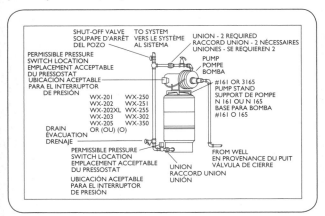

Figure 4.9 Typical Installation of a Vertical Pump-Stand Model Pressure Tank

(Courtesy of Amtrol, Inc.)

and allows you to mount a jet pump to it. Figure 4.8 shows an example of this type of installation for a horizontal tank. Figure 4.9 illustrates a pump stand tank that is set vertically.

MOUNTING A VERTICAL STAND-MODEL PRESSURE TANK

Mounting a vertical stand-model pressure tank is done on a solid, level surface. The tank is sometimes mounted on raised blocks to protect it in the event that the basement in which it is installed floods. The tank must be fully supported. These tanks can be used with both jet pumps and submersible pumps. Figure 4.10 shows a stand model used with a jet pump, and Figure 4.11 shows a stand model used with a submersible pump.

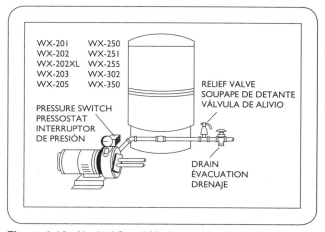

Figure 4.10 Vertical Stand Model Working with a Jet Pump
(Courtesy of Amtrol, Inc.)

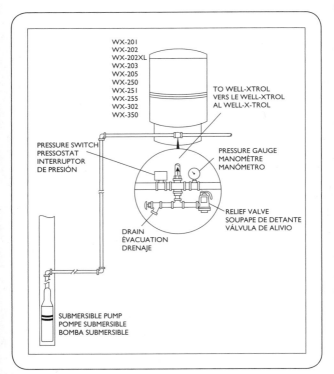

Figure 4.11 Vertical Stand Model Working with a Submersible Pump

(Courtesy of Amtrol, Inc.)

UNDERGROUND WELL PRESSURE TANKS

Underground well pressure tanks must be installed vertically. They must be protected from freezing. This is usually accomplished by installing the tanks below the frost line. The tanks are generally surrounded by coarse sand that is free of all rocks. See Figure 4.12 for an example of this type of installation.

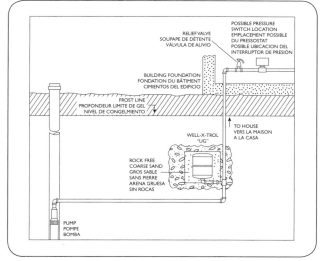

Figure 4.12 Typical Installation of an Underground Well Pressure Tank

(Courtesy of Amtrol, Inc.)

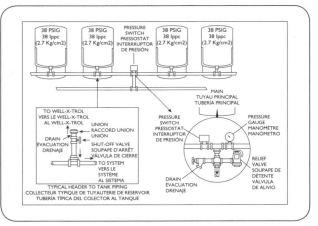

Figure 4.13 The Manifold Installation of Water Pressure Tanks

(Courtesy of Amtrol, Inc.)

MANIFOLD INSTALLATIONS

Manifold installations of multiple tanks are used when the water demands require it. In this type of installation the volume of water on hand can be increased substantially. Figure 4.13 shows how a manifold installation is executed.

The illustrations in this section show how pressure tanks are mounted and the normal piping arrangements.

FINE-TUNING YOUR INSTALLATION

Fine-tuning your installation is the last step in installing a pressure tank. This takes place when the pump, electrical wiring, and all piping and fittings have been installed to connect the pressure tank to the water distribution system.

Once the pump has filled the tank with water and cut off, you should have the desired water pressure showing on the pressure gauge that serves the pressure tank. Assuming this is the case, you need to verify the cut-in and cut-out functions of the pressure switch. Open a plumbing faucet. I normally use one that fills a bathtub to avoid flooding the fixture as I move back and forth between the faucet and the pressure tank. If the pressure switch is set properly you should not notice any pause in water delivery and the water pressure should remain acceptable at all times. If there is a pause in getting water, it is time to adjust the pressure switch.

Keep in mind that there are hot electrical wires in a pressure switch. Once you remove the protective housing that covers the switch you must be careful not to come into contact with the live wires. You will see a large spring with a nut securing the top of it. You can control cut-in and cut-out pressure by adjusting the retaining nut and either compressing the spring or releasing tension on the spring. Turn the adjustment device clockwise if you want to increase the cut-out pressure. If you turn the adjustment device counterclockwise you will decrease the cut-out pressure. This allows you to fine-tune the switch to provide optimum performance. See Figure 4.14 for an example of this type of pressure switch.

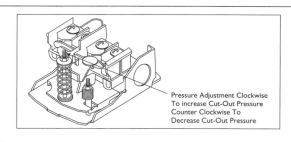

Pressure Adjustment Clockwise
To increase Cut-Out Pressure
Counter Clockwise To
Decrease Cut-Out Pressure

Figure 4.14　Adjusting a Pressure Switch

(continued)

ADJUSTING PRECHARGE

Prior to Installation

Step 1. Remove protective air valve cap

*Step 2. Check precharge pressure (pressure should be + or –
10% of the factory setting)*

*Step 3. Release or add air as necessary to make the precharge
pressure 2 psig below the pressure switch pump cut-in setting.
(Example, if you have a WX-202XL with a precharge of 38
psig, and you have a pressure switch setting of 30/50 psig,
adjust precharge of your WX-202XL from 38 psig to 28 psig.)*

*Step 4. Replace protective air valve cap. Peel off backing of label
and apply over air valve cap.*

START UP

Fine Tuning Procedures

*Many times the actual pressure switch will vary from the standard
pressure range indicated. These variations could cause a momentary lag of water delivery, as the pressure switch is not "tuned to
the WELL-X-TROL precharge pressure".*

1. *Fill the system and WELL-X-TROL until pump cuts off.*
2. *Open one or more fixtures to drain the WELL-X-TROL.*
3. *If there is a momentary pause in the water flow from the time
   the WELL-X-TROL is emptied and the pump starts, adjust
   pump cut-in setting clockwise slightly.*
4. *Close fixtures and refill WELL-X-TROL to pump cut off. Check
   time to fill.*
5. *Open fixtures and see if pause in water is eliminated. If not,
   continue adjusting pressure switch.*

ADJUSTING PRECHARGE AFTER INSTALLATION

*Step 1. Drain tank of all water. Check precharge pressure in the
WELL-X-TROL Tank.*

*Step 2. Release or add air as necessary to make the recharge
pressure 2 psig below the pressure switch pump cut-in setting.*

All WELL-X-TROL "Underground Tanks" *are designed for direct burial and must be installed in the vertical position* **only.** *To eliminate danger of freezing, tank should be buried below the frost line.*

The following steps should be taken when installing WELL-X-TROL "Underground Tanks":

1. *Make sure that the tank will be buried below the frost line and above the water table.*
2. *Remove plastic bag and check tank precharge. Factory precharge is 38 psig. Replace air stem cap securely. Follow adjusting precharge procedure.*
3. *Important: Install tank on firm rock-free earth.*
4. *The Water lines from the pump to the tank and switch location should be the same size to prevent switch cycling.*
5. *Check the system for performance and inspect for leaks.*
6. *Important: Backfill hole with sand. Firmly tamp fill to prevent settling. Failure to do so will shorten tank life.*
7. *Fill out pressure tank location sticker and affix to power panel or other visible surface so tank can be easily located at a later time*

(Courtesy of Amtrol, Inc.)

The installation of a pressure tank is not difficult once you understand the procedures used to select, size, mount, and plumb up the tank.

5

WELL PIPING CHOICES

Piping choices for getting water from a pump to a distribution system are plentiful. However, there are only three types of piping that are commonly used in modern well systems. Each type comes with its pros and cons.

The three primary types of piping used as a water service from a pump to a pressure tank are:

- Polyethylene (PE)
- Copper
- Cross-linked polybutylene (PEX)

Other types of piping may be used, but they are not primary choices. For example, it is acceptable to install galvanized steel piping for both a water service application and a water distribution application, but that type of pipe has not been used in many plumbing installations for decades. This chapter focuses on the three primary types of piping.

POLYETHYLENE PIPE (PE)

Polyethylene pipe is a plastic pipe. It is sold in rolls that range from about 100 feet to several hundred feet in length, which is excellent when this type of pipe is used as a water service because it can be run for long distances without any need for underground fittings to join sections of piping.

Polyethylene pipe is very affordable. It is easy to work with in moderate temperatures, but when the outside temperature is cold the pipe becomes stiff and more difficult to control. This makes installation of the piping a bit more difficult, and it may be necessary to warm the piping slightly to enable fittings and clamps to make solid connections in cold weather.

Polyethylene piping is subject to kinking if it is bent too far. This is a negative feature, but with proper handling it is rarely a serious concern. Since the pipe is made of plastic, it is subject to damage from punctures and crushing. As with any water service piping, all backfilling of trenches must be done with clean material that is free of sharp rocks, and the dirt should be installed in shallow layers so that the pipe is not crushed. In other words, it is not a good idea to dump an entire bucketload of dirt from a backhoe directly onto the piping. Furthermore, the bottom of the trench should be clean of debris and maintain a smooth service. Dips, holes, and other unusual conditions can cause kinking of the water service pipe during backfilling.

When handled and installed properly PE piping is fine for use between a well pump and a well pressure tank, but that is where the pipe must terminate. Since PE pipe is not rated for use with hot water, it is not an approved water distribution pipe and cannot be used in a water distribution system that includes hot-water piping.

Fittings for PE pipe can be made out of either metallic materials or nylon materials. Both are approved, but the metal fittings are less likely to break, and they are the choice of most professional plumbers.

Joints between fittings and PE pipe are made with insert fittings and stainless steel hose clamps. It is wise to use two clamps on each connection point. To make a joint, slide two clamps over the end of the pipe, then push the barbed insert fitting into the open end of the pipe. At this point, place the clamps over the barbed portion of the fitting and tighten the clamps.

A torque wrench is my favorite tool for tightening the clamps. The hub on the wrench fits the hex head on a clamp. The torque wrench clicks to alert you that the clamp is tight. This prevents you from stripping the clamps by overtightening, and it is a lot faster and easier than using a screwdriver to tighten them.

In cold weather you may find that the pipe is very stiff. This can make it difficult to insert a fitting, and clamps may not bite down hard enough on the barbed fittings. To compensate for this you can use a heat gun, a blow-dryer, or even a torch, if you have a good touch with it, to soften the pipe. Avoid using too much heat because the pipe will melt. You do not want to weaken the pipe with excessive heat. Your goal should be to make the pipe supple enough for the clamps to squeeze the pipe and hold it to the fitting.

Polyethylene pipe is sold in different pressure ratings. The minimum pressure rating that is recommended is 100 psi. This is normally adequate, but if you will have excessive pressure you should upgrade to a stronger version. I prefer a pipe that is rated for 160 psi.

COPPER

Copper has long been used for plumbing systems. It is an excellent piping material that has proved to have a long, useful life. However, the cost of copper is something to seriously consider. Copper is very expensive when compared to other acceptable piping materials.

A potential drawback of using copper piping as a water service is when a well contains acidic water. The acid can eat pinholes in the copper over time. This, of course, results in leaks. Some ground conditions can also affect the life of copper piping. Corrosive soils can do a lot of damage to metallic piping.

Long runs of copper tubing require the use of couplings. These fittings must be of a mechanical type. This is never desirable in an underground installation. Copper tubing does kink during some installations, and the wall thickness of the piping is subject to punctures when buried in a trench.

Copper is an expensive option for a water service pipe. It is still used, but plastic piping is far more common.

CROSS-LINKED POLYBUTYLENE (PEX)

PEX piping is sold in rolls that range from 100 feet on up. When it is used as a water service pipe there is rarely a need for the installation of fittings. Unlike PE piping, PEX piping is approved for water distribution piping.

PEX is a tough material. It can take a lot of abuse before it fails. The pipe is very flexible, which eliminates the need for most fittings when doing an installation below grade. Another plus to PEX is that it can expand considerably under freezing conditions without rupturing. This is not the case with copper or PE piping.

The price of PEX piping is far lower than that of copper and a little more than that of PE piping. The fittings used with PEX are barbed insert fittings. They are available in plastic and metal. I recommend using metal fittings.

There are two ways of making joints with PEX tubing. I prefer the use of crimp rings that are designed specifically for use with PEX piping and fittings. The rings are crimped with special tools. When connections are made properly, they are extremely secure and durable.

The other method of joining PEX piping is to employ thermal expansion and shrinking of the piping on the barbed fitting. This requires the use of a special piece of equipment to make the joints. Basically, the pipe is heated and a fitting is placed inside of it. As the pipe cools, it grips the barbs on the fitting to create a solid joint.

Both methods of joining PEX pipe are acceptable. I have been plumbing so long that I was using polybutylene piping back in the late 1970s. Polybutylene and PEX are very similar, but PEX is the better piping. Having cut my teeth on the method using crimp rings and crimping tools, I have never switched to the thermal system. This is just my personal decision, however; either method will provide secure joints.

WHICH PIPE?

Which type of piping will you use for your well system? In my experience most installers use PE piping as the water service and then convert to PEX piping at the water distribution system. This is normally the way I pipe a system, and I have not experienced any unusual problems with my systems.

Copper is just too expensive when bidding jobs on a competitive basis. Also, copper is a little harder to work with than the plastic piping options. Unless there are some special circumstances that warrant the use of copper, it is probably more likely that plastic piping will be installed.

PIPING SPECIFICATIONS

Access to piping specifications will be helpful to you when you are choosing water service pipe. The smallest diameter for water service pipe for normal conditions is .75 inch. A diameter of 1 inch is more common and is preferable. The price difference between the two is not a lot, and the larger pipe provides greater water volume and the option to expand the plumbing system without having to update the size of the water service. See Table 5.1 for a comparison of specifications for PE pipe.

Table 5.1 Specifications for PE Piping

Pressure Rating	Size (in inches)	Inside Diameter	Minimum Wall Thickness
100 psi	.75	.824	.060
	1	1.049	.070
	1.25	1.380	.092
125 psi	.75	.662	.060
	1	.824	.072
	1.25	1.049	.092
160 psi	.75	.824	.092
	1	1.049	.117
	1.25	1.380	.153

If you choose to install copper tubing as the water service, you will need to use either Type L copper or Type K copper. The rating has to do with the wall thickness of the piping. Rigid copper tubing and pipe is sold in 20-foot lengths, but this is not a suitable choice for water service. Coiled copper is the type of material used in the installation of copper water services. Type K copper is sold in 100-foot rolls up through the pipe size of 1.25 inches. This is also true of Type L copper.

See Tables 5.2 and 5.3 for listings of wall thickness for both Type L and Type K copper tubing.

Table 5.2 Wall Thickness of Type L Coiled Copper Tubing

Inside Diameter (in inches)	Outside Diameter (in inches)	Wall Thickness (in inches)
3/4	7/8	0.641
1	1 1/8	0.839
1.25	1 3/8	1.04

Table 5.3 Wall Thickness of Type K Coiled Copper Tubing

Inside Diameter (in inches)	Outside Diameter (in inches)	Wall Thickness (in inches)
3/4	7/8	0.455
1	1 1/8	0.655
1.25	1 3/8	0.042

PEX tubing has a pressure rating of 100 psi at 180°F. The pressure rating is 160 psi at 74°F. PEX tubing with a diameter of .75 inch has a wall thickness of 0.070 inch. The recommended circuit length for PEX with a .75-inch diameter is 500 feet, and the maximum circuit length is 600 feet. When you move up to a 1-inch diameter, the recommended circuit length is 750 feet. This is also the maximum circuit length. Obviously, you can install a long run of piping without fittings when working with PEX tubing.

SOME INSTALLATION POINTERS

Now you know something about the piping choices for water services. Here are a few installation pointers that may save you a lot of headaches in the future. The following suggestions are based on the plumbing code and my personal experiences over the last 30 years.

- You can often install a pipe with a .75-inch diameter as a water service, but I prefer to use 1-inch pipe to provide for future usage needs.
- PE piping is the common choice for use as a water service.
- Size the water service pipe based on the plumbing requirements that must be met.
- The trench used to house the water service should be clean of debris and sharp objects. The floor of the trench should be fairly even to prevent crushing or crimping the piping during the backfilling process.
- Make sure that the water service you are installing is below the frost line for your region.
- Use only approved fittings and connections for underground piping.
- Backfill material should be installed in layers. It is common to install about 6 inches of fill at a time. This is normally compacted before the next layer is added.
- When the water service is installed in a trench that contains a sewer, some special provisions must be made. Normally, this amounts to providing a solid shelf above the sewer on one side of the trench to house the water service. When this is not possible, the water service should be separated from the sewer with a dirt barrier that is 5 feet wide and compacted.
- Inspect all piping carefully for kinks prior to backfilling a trench.
- Record the location and depth of the water service in the event that it needs to be excavated for repairs in the future.
- Put a pressure test on the piping before it is buried. Even new piping can have leaks in it.
- Use gentle bends when making a change in direction with water service piping.
- It is normal for the installation of a water service to require inspection by a code enforcement officer. Make sure this is done prior to burying the pipe.

This concludes our look at piping choices for water services. Once you get the water service into a building, you must begin to install the components that make up the rest of the well system. Chapter 6 introduces you to the various elements used in the installation of well systems.

WELL SYSTEM COMPONENTS

There is a multitude of components used in well systems. The devices vary, depending on whether a jet pump or a submersible pump is used. Some components can be used in both types of well systems. The purpose here is to introduce you to the many types of parts and fittings that will be used when installing or servicing a well system.

The equipment used in well systems includes the following:

- Check valves
- Gate valves
- Ball valves
- Foot valves
- Relief valves
- Pressure gauges
- Pressure switches
- Boiler drains
- Torque arrestor
- Pitless adapter
- Tail pipe
- Well rope
- Tank tee
- Unions
- Pipe
- Fittings
- Pumps
- Pressure tanks
- Electrical controls

This is a rundown of the common elements that may be installed in a well system. Now let's take a look at what they do and when you will use them.

MAJOR COMPONENTS

The major components that are needed for a suitable well system are well pumps and pressure tanks. Both of these components have already been described, so they are only mentioned here. The same is true of pipes and fittings. We are now ready to move on to the additional requirements for a good well system.

CHECK VALVES

Check valves are needed to keep the pump from running constantly. If a check valve is not installed, the water in the water service drops back into the well when the pump stops running. This triggers the pump to run again. A pump can be worn out very quickly under these conditions.

In the case of a jet pump, the foot valve acts as a check valve. When installing a submersible pump, the check valve is a brass fitting that is installed in-line in the piping to the pressure tank. Make sure you don't install these valves backward. If you do, no water comes to the tank. There is an arrow cast into the side of the valve that shows the proper direction for installing the valve. Install the check valve so that the arrow is pointing toward the pressure tank and not toward the pump.

Water will pass through the check valve easily. When the pump stops running, the check valve closes and holds the water in place. This is a simple, inexpensive component, but it is a critical one.

GATE VALVES

Gate valves or ball valves need to be installed in the well piping near the well pressure tank (see Figure 6.1). The shutoff valve needs to be of a positive-closing type, such as a gate or ball valve. Do not install stop-and-waste valves that depend on rubber washers to operate properly. The other reason for using a full-open valve is to allow full water flow to the pressure tank. A stop-and-waste valve restricts water flow due to the design of the valve.

Figure 6.1 Gate Valve

FOOT VALVES

Foot valves are installed on the drop pipe that extends from a jet pump into well water. It is equipped with a strainer and acts as a check valve. These valves are not used with submersible pumps. A foot valve normally attaches directly to the pipe that resides in a pump. They are used with both shallow-well jet pumps and deep-well jet pumps.

RELIEF VALVES

Relief valves protect pressure tanks from building excessive pressure. This valve is installed either on piping attached to a jet pump or on a tank tee when a submersible pump is installed. If excessive pressure builds in the pressure tank, the relief valve opens and discharges the pressure to keep the system safe.

Table 6.1 Factory Settings for Relief Valves to Open

Relief Valve Diameter (in inches)	Open Pressure Setting
½	75 psi
¾	75 psi
1	75 psi
1¼	65 psi
1½	65 psi

PRESSURE GAUGES

Pressure gauges are needed to monitor water pressure in a well system. Most of these gauges have a maximum rating of 100 psi or 125 psi. They can be installed directly on a jet pump or on a tank tee when a submersible pump is installed.

PRESSURE SWITCHES

Pressure switches are used to control the points at which a pump cuts on and off. The switches come with different ratings. A low-pressure gauge has the pump cut on and pump when water pressure drops to 20 psi and cut off when the pressure reaches 40 psi. Another model cuts on at 30 psi and off at 50 psi. You can also get a switch that cuts off at 60 psi and cuts on at 40 psi. These are the typical options used. Other switches can operate at higher pressures.

BOILER DRAINS

Boiler drains are installed at a low point on piping at a pressure tank. They are often installed on tank tees. These valves allow water to be drained out of a pressure tank when service or repair is required. There should be a full-open valve on the inlet piping to a pressure tank. A second full-open valve should be installed on the outlet pipe from the tank as the piping proceeds to make a water distribution system. When both of these valves are closed, they isolate the tank. This allows the boiler drain to be used to drain only the pressure tank.

TORQUE ARRESTORS

Torque arrestors are installed on the drop piping when installing submersible pumps. This is a very simple device that provides protection for the well pipe. The torque arrestor is made of rubber. It slides over the well pipe, then it is compressed by pushing the two ends of the device toward each other, which makes the rubber expand out. When the rubber protector is at the proper diameter, clamps are tightened on each end of the torque arrestor. The clamps maintain the compression.

When a well pipe is installed in a drilled well, the torque arrestor keeps the pipe from bouncing into the well casing as a pump starts and stops. This prevents potential damage from abrasion on the piping. These devices are not required, but they are strongly recommended.

PITLESS ADAPTERS

Pitless adapters are used with drilled wells and submersible pumps. The adapter allows the water service pipe to connect to the drop pipe in the well. A hole is drilled in the well casing at a depth equal to the depth of the water service. Pitless adapters are designed to create a watertight connection on the side of the well casing. Once the adapter is installed and connected to the water service, the pump, piping, and wires can be lowered into the well. This is done by attaching part of the pitless adapter to the drop pipe. Then that part of the adapter must be placed into the main housing of the adapter. This is normally done with a well tee. We will talk more about this in Chapter 9. Once the pitless adapter is fitted together there is a watertight seal and the drop pipe is connected to the water service.

TAIL PIPES

Tail pipes are not normally used. However, they are installed with jet pumps when wells have low recovery rates. This component is used with deep-well jet pumps. The tail pipe attaches to the well piping where a foot valve would normally be installed. Tail pipes can vary in length, but they are usually 20 to 30 feet long. A foot valve is installed on the end of a tail pipe.

When this type of arrangement is used, it keeps the foot valve deep enough to help prevent pumping a well dry. They are not needed for most wells, but if you are working with a well that has a weak recovery rate, the installation of a tail pipe can make the difference between success and failure when it comes to dependable water delivery.

WELL ROPE

Well rope is an optional component, but it is senseless not to use it when installing a submersible pump. The process is simple. Tie one end of the nylon rope tightly to the pump. Measure out the amount of rope needed to reach from the installed pump location to several feet above the top of the well casing. Before you lower the submersible pump into a well, tie the upper end of the rope tightly around the well casing on the outside of the well.

Why would you use a well rope? If you drop the well piping, you can lose the pump in a deep well. Likewise, when a fitting breaks in a well, the pump can be lost. This is an expensive loss. If a pump becomes separated from the drop pipe or if the pipe itself is dropped, the rope will save the pump. Installing a well rope adds a few dollars to the cost of an installation, but it is very cheap insurance. Any plumber or pump installer who has been in the field over the years has stories to tell about pumps that were lost and unrecoverable.

TANK TEES

Tank tees are great. They install directly into a well pressure tank and are tapped to accept all the fittings and components needed to make a working well system. The tees are made of brass and keep all of the controls, devices, and equipment in one convenient location. You can pipe a system without a tank tee, but the added expense of the part saves a lot of time and effort for the installer.

UNIONS

Unions are installed on both the inlet and the outlet piping of pressure tanks. On the inlet pipe there should be a full-open valve in front of the union. The cut-off valve on the outlet piping should be installed between the union and the water distribution system. When this is the case, the valves can be closed, a boiler drain can be used to drain a pressure tank, and the unions can be opened to make the replacement of a defective tank easy.

ELECTRICAL DEVICES

Electrical devices are a part of any well system. They include a pressure switch. A disconnect control is usually installed near the well pump in the case of a jet pump or near a pressure tank when a submersible pump is used. Heat-shrink devices are used to protect electrical connections that will be lowered into well water. We will go into more detail on electrical components and their associated needs in Chapter 7.

This completes an overview of the common components used in well systems. In Chapters 8 and 9 you will learn how these components are installed. It is important to understand what the devices do and why they are used. Chapter 7 delves into electrical facts and figures.

7

ELECTRICAL FACTS AND FIGURES

Electrical facts and figures come into play in the installation of well systems. The process is different for jet pumps than it is for submersible pumps. All electrical wiring is above ground for jet pumps. This is not the case with submersible pumps. When a submersible pump is installed, wiring goes right down into the well water. Obviously, the electrical connections must be properly protected from any form of water invasion.

Major electrical work is normally done by licensed electricians. Pump installers and plumbers are allowed to do some electrical wiring, but they are limited in their ability to meet electrical needs for a well system.

In theory, the electrical work is pretty cut and dried. It begins at a power panel or subpanel and makes its way to the pump and pressure switch. The power source can be protected by simple circuit breakers. A dedicated control box or disconnect box can be installed. This is more often the case with jet pumps. It is best to leave this part of the job to a licensed electrician.

Before discussing the types of work that installers and plumbers normally do with electrical wiring, take note of Tables 7.1 and 7.2, which you can use for reference when performing this kind of work. The tables are self-explanatory.

Table 7.1 Electrical Data for Control Panel Enclosures

Enclosure Rating	Explanation
NEMA 1 General Purpose	To prevent accidental contact with enclosed apparatus. Suitable for application indoors where not exposed to unusual service conditions,
NEMA 2 Driptight	To prevent accidental contact, and in addition, to exclude failing moisture or dirt.
NEMA 3 Weatherproof (Weatherproof Rraintight)	Protection against specified weather hazards. Suitable for use outdoors.
NEMA3 R Raintight	Protects against entrance of water from a beating rain. Suitable for general outdoor application not requiring sleetproof.
NEMA 4 Watertight	Designed to exclude water applied in form of hose stream. To protect against stream of water during cleaning operations, etc.
NEMA 4X Watertight & Corrosion Resistant	Designed to exclude water applied in form of hose stream. To protect against stream of water during cleaning operations, etc. Corrosion Resistant,
NEMA 5 Dustight	Constructed so that dust will not enter enclosed case. Being replaced in some Dust Tight equipment by NEMA 12.
NEMA 6 Watertight, Dustight	Intended to permit enclosed apparatus to be operated successfully when temporarily submerged in water.

NEMA 7 Hazardous Locations Class I	Designed to meet application requirements of National Electrical Code for Class I, Hazardous Locations (explosive atmospheres). Circuit interruption occurs in air.
NEMA 8 Hazardous Locations A, B, C or D Class II – Oil Immersed	Identical to NEMA 7 above, except the apparatus is immersed in oil.
NEMA 9 Class II – Hazardous Locations	Designed to meet application requirements of National Electrical Code for Class II Hazardous Locations (combustible dusts, etc), E, F and G,
NEMA 10 Bureau of Mines Permissible	Meets requirements of U.S. Bureau of Mines. Suitable for use in coal mines.
NEMA 11 Dripproof Corrosion Resistant	Provides oil immersion of apparatus such that it is suitable for application where equipment is subject to acid or other corrosive fumes,
MEMA12 Driptight, Dusttight	For use in those industries where it is desired to exclude dust, lint, fibers and flyings, or oil or industrial coolant seepage,

(Courtesy of Goulds Pumps)

Table 7.2 Jet Pump Motor Data

HP	Volts	Phase	Service Factor	Max. Load Amps	Watts	Circuit Breaker	Switch®
1/2	115/230	1	1.6	10.8/5.4	880	25/15	629002 2
3/4	115/230	1	1.5	14.8/7.4	1280	30/15	629002 2
1	115/230	1	1.4	16.2/8.1	1440	30/20	629002 2
1½	115/230	1	1.3	20.0/10.0	1866	40/20	629002 2
2	115/230	1	1.2	22.6/11.3	2100	25/15	629002 2
3	230	1	1.15	13.3	3280	30	629002 2
1/2	115/230	1	1.6	10.8/5.4	968	25/15	629002 2
3/4	115/230	1	1.5	14.8/7.4	1336	30/15	629002 2
1	115/230	1	1.4	16.2/8.1	1592	30/20	629002 2
1½	115/230	1	1.3	21.4/10,7	1950	40/20	629002 2
2	230	1	1.2	12.9	2100	25	629002 2
1/2	115/230	1	1.6	9.4/4.7	900	20/10	3945C91A01
3/4	115/230	1	1.5	13.6/6.8	1160	25/15	3945C91A01
1	115/230	1	1.4	15.8/7.9	1400	30/20	3945C91A01
1/2	115/230	1	1.6	12.6/6.3	990	25/15	629002 2
3/4	115/230	1	1.5	14.8/7.4	1200	30/15	629002 2
1	115/230		1.4	16.2/8.1	1400	30/20	629002 2

(Courtesy of Goulds Pumps)

Electricians handle all elements of wiring and electrical connection on some jobs, but there are also jobs for which they run a feed wire to either a jet pump or a wellhead and leave the rest to a plumber or pump installer. Who does what depends largely on code regulations in various local jurisdictions.

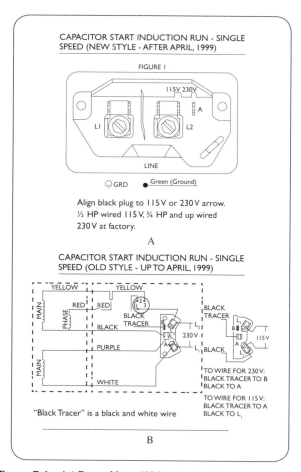

Figure 7.1 Jet Pump Motor Wiring for A. O. Smith Motors
(Courtesy of Goulds Pumps)

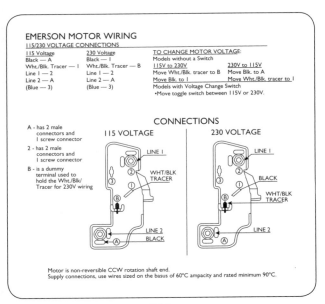

Figure 7.2 Emerson Motor Wiring

(Courtesy of Goulds Pumps)

Plumbers and pump installers are normally allowed to work with existing electrical wiring when troubleshooting and repairing a well system. In some regions only licensed electricians are allowed to make new installations. Before you do any electrical work, make sure that your trade license and liability insurance covers you for the type of work to be done. And, of course, be certain that the wires you are working with on new installations are not energized with electrical power.

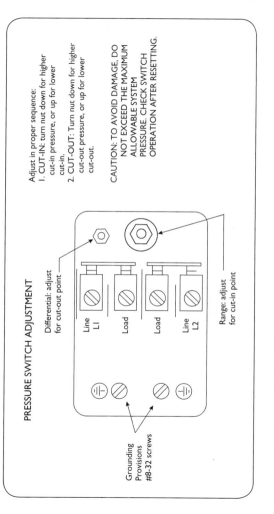

PRESSURE SWITCH ADJUSTMENT

Adjust in proper sequence:
1. CUT-IN: turn nut down for higher cut-in pressure, or up for lower cut-in.
2. CUT-OUT: Turn nut down for higher cut-out pressure, or up for lower cut-out.

CAUTION: TO AVOID DAMAGE, DO NOT EXCEED THE MAXIMUM ALLOWABLE SYSTEM PRESSURE. CHECK SWITCH OPERATION AFTER RESETTING.

Differential: adjust for cut-out point

Range: adjust for cut-in point

Line L1

Load

Load

Line L2

Grounding Provisions #8-32 screws

Figure 7.3 Pressure Switch Adjustment
(Courtesy of Goulds Pumps)

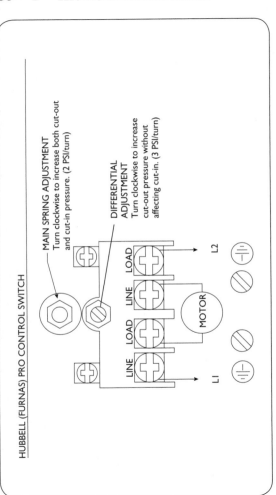

Figure 7.4 Pressure Switch Wiring for Hubbell Pro Control switch
(Courtesy of Goulds Pumps)

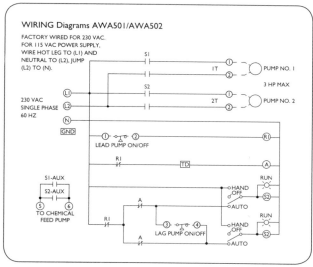

Figure 7.5 Example of a Wiring Diagram
(Courtesy of Goulds Pumps)

TIP: Never trust an electrical switch. I made this mistake once with an electric water heater earlier in my career.

I pulled the main fuses in the house and started to remove the electrical wires.

After a surprising and shocking experience, I found that the water heater had a separate electrical source on the outside of the house.

Cut the power off based on the switch or circuit breaker. Then check the wire with an electrical meter to be sure that the wire is not carrying electricity.

Because of my early experience with electrical work, I now use two meters to check wires to ensure that one of them is not broken.

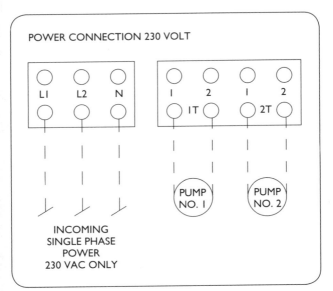

Figure 7.6 Example of a Wiring Diagram for a 230-Volt Pump
(Courtesy of Goulds Pumps)

MANUFACTURER'S RECOMMENDATIONS

Always follow the manufacturer's recommendations when installing a well system. Pay particular attention to this with the electrical wiring. Confirm that the voltage coming to the pump wiring is the proper amount. Mixing up a 115-volt system with a 230-volt system is not going to work.

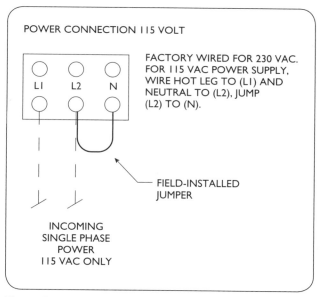

Figure 7.7 Example of a Wiring Diagram for a 115-Volt Pump
(Courtesy of Goulds Pumps)

CONNECTING THE PRESSURE SWITCH

Connecting the pressure switch to the wiring supply is not difficult. I have provided examples of how this is done. The advantage in installing jet pumps is that all the wiring is located at the pump.

When wiring must enter a hole for access to connection points, you need to install a stress-relief insert. This is simply a round device that has a threaded portion that fits through the hole. The device is held in place with a nut that screws on from the inside of the hole. Once the nut is threaded onto the stress-relief insert, you can feed the wiring cable though the insert.

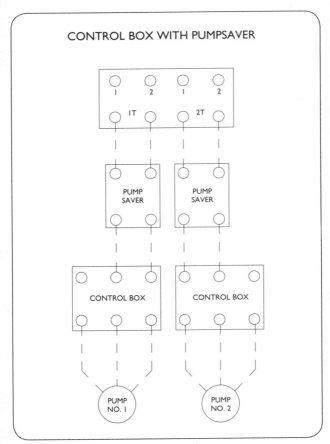

Figure 7.8 Optional Centripro Control Box and Pumpsaver
(Courtesy of Goulds Pumps)

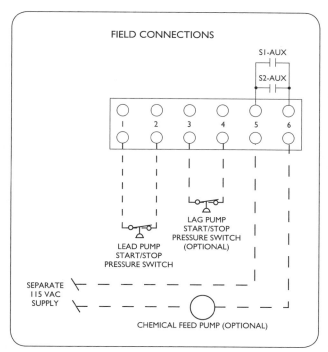

Figure 7.9 Example of a Wiring Diagram for Field Connections

(Courtesy of Goulds Pumps)

A stress-relief clamp is located on the outside of the wiring hole. This is a metal strip below which the wiring cable is installed. Once enough cable is in the hole, tighten two screws on the bar, which provides pressure on the electrical cable. This prevents wiring connections from being dislodged accidentally by pulling on the cable.

Wires must be stripped of their insulation to be installed under the nuts of a pressure switch. Once this is done, the copper wiring is installed under the connection point and then the securing nut is tightened. The tightening is done by turning the connection point clockwise. For this reason, you should bend a small crook in the wire and install it with the crooked end positioned so that clockwise tension will tighten the wire. If you install the bent end of the wire in the other direction, the turning of the connection point creates a tendency for the wire to come off the connection stud.

There are two main wires and a ground wire to secure. The ground wire is installed under a green screw near the connection point. Confirm which wires are installed under which connection points on the switch. This information is identified in the paperwork that comes with the type of switch you are working with. Normally the red wire is the hot wire and the black wire is the neutral wire, but don't make this assumption automatically. Check the manufacturer's recommendations to ensure that you are connecting the wires properly.

WIRING FOR SUBMERSIBLE PUMPS

Wiring for a submersible pump is buried in a trench and submerged in well water. It is common for an electrician to install the wiring in a trench to the point where it meets the wellhead. The wiring in the trench is turned up and placed inside conduit to protect it. Submersible well caps are formed to allow the wiring to enter the well casing. An electrician may take the wiring to this point.

When the time comes to install a submersible pump, the work is done above ground before the pump is submerged. This is sometimes accomplished by stretching well pipe out on the ground and connecting the pump to it. People who install pumps regularly use a pump well on the back of their trucks to hold the well pipe. This allows them to feed the piping out as they need to.

Once the pump is installed on the drop pipe, the wiring can be installed. Most submersible pumps use a three-wire system. Again, confirm voltage requirements and use the information provided by the pump manufacturer for the installation. You may be able to run your wiring the full length of the drop pipe without coupling it, which is the preferred way to do it.

Electrical wiring is taped to the drop pipe at close intervals to prevent the wiring from hanging loosely in the well. Electrical tape is normally used for this. It is important to prevent the wiring from coming into contact with the well casing. If it does rub on the casing, the insulation can be chafed and create problems that will necessitate pulling the pump to replace the wiring.

When the pump, its pipe, and its wiring are lowered into the well, you need to keep the piping from sliding over the top edge of the well casing. This can damage both the piping and the wiring. Guide the pump assembly down the center of the well casing to prevent any scraping damage.

When the wiring reaches the wellhead from inside the well, it has to be connected to the feed wires that come into the casing from the trench. This is done with waterproof, heat-shrink connectors.

Heat-shrink connectors have a plastic sleeve and metal connection points. First, the insulation is stripped from the ends of the wiring. The wires are placed into the connector so that they are both fully under the connection points. Then the thin metal connectors are squeezed shut to secure the wiring.

Once the wires are under the connectors, you are ready to heat-shrink the coupling. This is best done with a heat gun or a blow-dryer. The plastic sleeves extend past the connectors and encircle the insulated wiring. When you apply heat, the plastic melts and fuses together. This makes the connection waterproof when it is done properly.

We have covered the basics of wiring for new pump installations. We will go into more detail about electrical connections in Chapter 12, which deals with troubleshooting.

> *TIP: Never use wire nuts to connect wires that may come into contact with wet or damp conditions. Always use waterproof heat-shrink connectors.*

8

JET PUMP INSTALLATIONS

Jet pump installations pertain to both single-pipe and two-pipe jet pumps. You may deal with both new installations and replacements. Previous chapters examined different elements of jet pumps. By now you know the basics about the types of equipment used in the installation of jet pumps, as well as having some familiarity with the procedures involved. This chapter considers a new installation from start to finish, then takes a look at replacement work.

Chapter 2 described the types of pumps you can choose from for a well system. The sizing requirements were also discussed. Refer to Chapter 2 for this type of information, although this chapter supplies a little of it as a refresher course. For information on selecting and sizing pressure tanks, see Chapter 4.

Tables 8.1 and 8.2 list some of the common water requirements for plumbing systems.

Table 8.1 Approximate Water Supply Requirements

Home Fixtures
Filling Ordinary Lavatory – 2 gal.
Filling avg, Bath Tub – 30 gal.
Flushing Water Closet – 6 gal.
Each Shower Bath – Up to 60 gal,
Dishwashing Machine – 15 gal./load
Automatic Laundry Machine – Up to 50 gal./load
Backwashing Domestic Water Softener – Up to 100 gal.

(Continued)

Table 8.1 *(Continued)*

Yard Fixtures
½″ Hose with Nozzle – 3 gpm
¼″ Hose with Nozzle – 5 gpm
Lawn Sprinkler – 2 gpm

(Courtesy of Goulds Pumps)

Table 8.2 Seven-Minute Peak Demand Period Usage

Performance Rating in Gallons per Minute			
Pump Discharge Pressure			
Total Suction Lift	**20 PSI**	**30 PSI**	**Max. Shut-Off in Lbs.**
5 feet	8 GPM	6 GPM	51 lbs.

(Courtesy of Goulds Pumps)

Figure 8.1 shows the rate of water flow needed when both a shower and a kitchen faucet are delivering water at the same time.

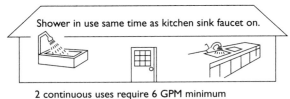

Shower in use same time as kitchen sink faucet on.

2 continuous uses require 6 GPM minimum
The capacity required of the pump is determined by the number of continuous use outlets in use at the same time. You can't use water at one or a number of outlets any faster than the pump supplies it.

Figure 8.1 Two Continuous Uses That Require 6-GPM Water Flow

(Courtesy of Goulds Pumps)

See the example provided for an example of the math necessary to compute the discharge demand on a pump.

Example

Service pressure desired – 30 lbs. minimum. . . . . .30 lbs.
Elevation 23 ft.
   1 lb. = 2.3 ft.
   23 ft./2.3 ft. = 10 lbs. . . . . .10 lbs.
Friction:
Pump capacity is 7 GPM
This flow through 200 ft. of 1" pipe
gives a friction loss of 3.06 lbs. . . . .<u>3 lbs.</u>
   43 lbs.
Pressure switch setting at the pump would be (43–63 lbs.)

(Courtesy of Goulds Pumps)

Figure 8.2 provides an example of how to determine the suction lift of a jet pump.

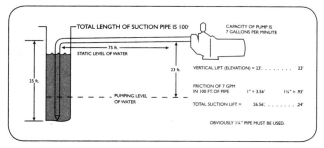

Figure 8.2 Example of Determining Suction Lift of a Jet Pump

(Courtesy of Goulds Pumps)

NEW INSTALLATION OF A SHALLOW-WELL JET PUMP

Once you have all your sizing facts and figures together, it is time to install a new shallow-well jet pump. We will assume that the well in question has a depth of about 30 feet. In this case you will be using PE piping for the drop pipe and the water service. The well is in place and the trench is open and allows for the installation of the water service below the local frost line.

Start your job by locating and setting the well pressure tank. Chapter 4 detailed the procedure for this task. The installation of the pump is taking place in the basement of a home. Figure 8.3 is a representative example of how this installation might look when it is complete.

After the pressure tank is set in place, you can put the pump in place as well. You might be using a pressure tank with a pump bracket that will hold the pump. Otherwise, you are likely to use a stand-model tank, as shown in Figure 8.4.

Once the pump is in place you can add the components on the pump, including the pressure switch that operates it. Review Chapter 6 if you need help remembering the types of components that are used.

Install a full-open valve on the piping that runs from the pump to the pressure tank. The more elements of the system that you can isolate, the easier it will be for service technicians to work on or replace the pump or pressure tank.

Figure 8.4 shows a close-up detail of a shallow-well jet pump.

It is advisable to install a full-open valve on the well pump before the water service is connected to the pump. You can use brass male and female adapters to make the transition for the valve to the PE piping. I recommend using metallic fittings for all joints in PE pipe. Remember that it is recommended that you install two stainless steel clamps to secure PE piping to each barb of a fitting.

Your water service piping may leave the home by being installed below the foundation footing. If the water service was not run into the home prior to the concrete floor being poured, this will not be possible. The alternative is to go through the foundation. This may mean making a hole in either a concrete wall or a cinder block wall. The construction

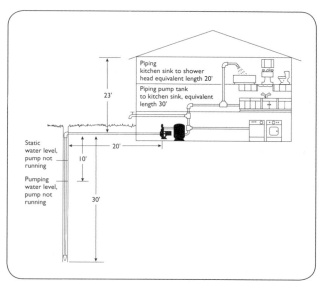

Figure 8.3 Representative Example of How a Shallow-Well Jet Pump Might Look

(Courtesy of Goulds Pumps)

Table 8.3 Seven-Minute Peak Demand Period Usage

Seven Minute Peak Demand Period Usage						
	Flow Rate GPM	Total Usage Gallons	Bathrooms In Home			
Outlets			1	1½	2-2½	3-4
Shower or Bath Tub	5	35	35	35	53	70
Lavatory	4	2	2	4	6	8
Toilet	4	5	5	10	15	20
Kitchen Sink	5	3	3	3	3	3
Automatic Washer	5	35	–	18	18	18
Dishwasher	2	14	–	–	3	3

(Continued)

			45	70	98	122
Normal seven minute*peak demand (gallons)			45	70	98	122
Minimum sized pump required to meet peak demand without supplemental supply			7 GPM (420)	10 GPM (600)	14 GPM (840)	17 GPM (1020)

Note: Values given are average and do not include higher or lower extremes.

*Peak demand can occur several times during morning and evening hours.

Additional Requirements: Farm, irrigation and sprinkling requirements are not shown. These values must be added to the peak demand figures if usage will occur during normal demand periods.

(Courtesy of Goulds Pumps)

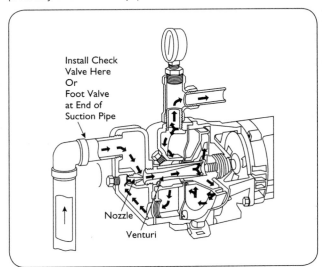

Figure 8.4 Detail of a Shallow-Well Jet Pump

(Courtesy of Goulds Pumps)

crew that formed and poured the walls should have installed a sleeve in the forms that would allow the concrete to flow around it, leaving a gap to give you unrestricted access to the water service trench.

A sleeve that is twice the diameter of the water service is required when penetrating a masonry wall. Sleeves are usually made of Schedule-40 PVC or ABS pipe. Once you have all the connections made, you will need to fill the annular space between the water service pipe and the sleeve. Many installers do this with expanding foam that is sprayed into the sleeve. Then a waterproof sealant is used on both the interior and the exterior faces of the wall. Do not seal the sleeve until all the connections have been made and tested. If you have to remove the piping for one reason or another, you will not want it held in place with expanding foam.

Make sure that the bottom of the trench is compacted and free of debris and sharp objects such as rocks. The water service runs from the valve at the pump to the interior of the well casing. This hole also needs to be sealed with some form of waterproof material.

The next step is to install the drop pipe and the foot valve. Once you know how long you want your well drop to be, you can cut a section of pipe and make it up with a foot valve on one end of it and a brass elbow on the other end. This elbow will be used to connect the drop pipe to the water service.

The discharge pipe from a pressure tank should be equipped with a full-open valve. You should also check the air charge in the pressure tank to make sure it is within a usable range. The home's water distribution piping will begin at the valve on the discharge side of the pressure tank. That is how you install a jet pump. Once all your well system components are in place and the electrical wiring is done, you can conduct a pressure test to make sure the system works properly. When you are sure that all is as it should be, seal the pipe sleeves, and you are done.

REPLACING A SHALLOW-WELL JET PUMP

If you know how to install a water pump, replacing one is not much of a challenge. Chapter 12 provides you with a host of troubleshooting techniques and information that will allow you to determine when a pump should be replaced. Here we will focus on the work required to make a successful replacement.

Once you have determined that a pump must be replaced, the logical starting point is choosing a new pump that is rated for the same performance as the existing pump. This, of course, assumes that a proper pump was installed in the first place.

Your work should begin by turning off the electrical power to the old pump. The next step is closing valves to isolate the pump from the water service and pressure tank. If an installer did not provide these valves, you should drain the pressure tank before you attempt to remove the pump.

Go ahead and remove the old pump. A new pump should fit in the same location. Piping connections may not be the same, but they are easy enough to modify. Once you have the pump in place and piped into the system, you need to decide whether you will reuse the old pump components or install new components. Some customers will want to save money by reusing parts such as a pressure gauge, relief valve, and pressure switch. This is not a good idea. You are responsible for the installation. If the old parts fail quickly after you have finished the job, you will probably have to replace them under warranty, without being paid for your time. I would insist on using all new components. Most reasonable people will accept this decision.

After all of the connections are made, you can open valves or close the drain valve on the pressure tank, turn on the electrical power, and test your installation. Once you are satisfied that the well system is working properly, you should open a plumbing faucet in a bathtub to remove any air that was trapped in the piping while it was cut apart. If you decide to purge the air through a kitchen faucet, remove the aerator before you turn the water on. The screen in the aerator could become clogged with debris if you leave it in place during the purging process. Replace the aerator once the system is running properly, and go back and check the well system connections again. If they are still solid, you should be done.

INSTALLATION OF A DEEP-WELL JET PUMP

The installation of a deep-well jet pump is very similar to that of a shallow-well pump. Therefore, we will only cover the differences in this section. Take notice of Figure 8.5 for a detailed view of a deep-well jet pump.

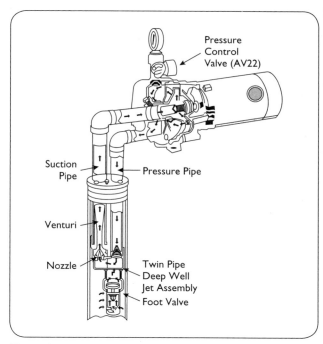

Figure 8.5 Detail of a Deep-Well Jet Pump
(Courtesy of Goulds Pumps)

Figure 8.6 illustrates typical installations of various types of jet pumps.

Shallow-well jet pumps use only a single pipe in the well installation. That pipe is a suction pipe. However, deep-well jet pumps use two pipes to enter the well. One of the pipes is a pressure pipe and the other one is a suction pipe. Due to the low lift required for a shallow-well jet pump, it can operate with only suction power. Deep wells require a jet pump that

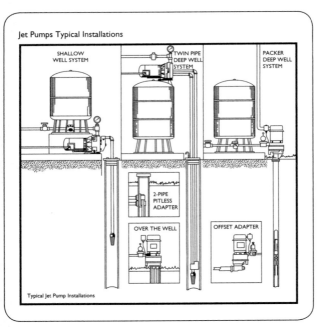

Figure 8.6 Typical Installations of Various Types of Jet Pumps

(Courtesy of Goulds Pumps)

pushes water down one pipe and pulls it up the other pipe to compensate for the added depth.

When the pipes from a deep-well jet pump reach a wellhead, they are typically installed either in through the top of the well cap or with the use of two pitless adapters that are installed in the side of the well casing. The use of pitless adapters is the more common of the two installations. As the pipes extend into the well, they are fitted with a twin-pipe jet assembly. The actual installation of the jet assembly and foot valve is done before the piping is lowered into a well. A foot valve is then attached to the jet assembly. In the case of a well with a low recovery rate, a section of tail pipe is installed between the jet assembly and the foot valve. This lowers the foot valve to compensate for the poor recovery rate of the well to prevent the well from being pumped below the level of the foot valve. (We discussed this in Chapter 3.)

Aside from the use of two pipes rather than one, the installation procedure is essentially the same for both shallow-well jet pumps and deep-well jet pumps. This is also true for the replacement of a two-pipe pump.

9

SUBMERSIBLE PUMP INSTALLATION

Submersible pump installation is taunting to some people. It shouldn't be. Installing a submersible pump requires many and various parts, but the process is straightforward. Many plumbers and installers prefer installing submersible pumps to installing jet pumps.

We talked about well pressure tanks in Chapter 4, which specified adequate installation in terms of sizing, selection, and installation requirements for pressure tanks. We talked about choosing submersible pumps in Chapter 3 and about electrical considerations in Chapter 7. Thus, there is no need to rehash that material here. The purpose of this chapter is to detail a normal installation for a submersible pump in a residential setting.

For our example, assume that the pressure tank is a stand model that will be installed in a residential home basement with a concrete floor. A licensed electrician has installed the pump's control box and run wires for the pressure switch and out of the house, down the pipe trench, to a point where the wires turn up at the well casing. An appropriate trench has been provided for you between the foundation of the home and the well casing. The concrete workers installed a sleeve in the concrete that will allow the piping and wires to leave the basement. You will take over the installation from this point and complete it.

Where to begin is often the first question that a rookie installer has about installing a submersible pump. If you were to lay out all the components used in such an installation, they would intimidate most people who were not experienced in pump installations. There are a lot of components used in a typical installation. I prefer to start at the wellhead, with the installation of a pitless adapter.

PITLESS ADAPTER

A pitless adapter is used in nearly all submersible pump installations. The adapter allows a horizontal water service pipe in a trench to be connected to it and converted to the vertical drop pipe that enters the well water. A watertight seal is created when a pitless adapter is installed properly. This is essential to maintain water quality in the well.

Before a pitless adapter can be installed, a hole must be made in the steel well casing. I use a hole saw on a drill to make the holes. A quality hole saw is required to get through the casing. The pilot bit that is part of the hole-saw assembly also must be of good quality. The casing material is hard, and cheap equipment will burn out and be rendered toothless before it cuts a hole.

Once the hole is open, the adapter can be installed. This is done by pushing the adapter through the hole from inside the well casing. The connection fittings are installed on the trench side of the fitting. Once the pitless adapter is in place, the rest of the work can continue.

There is no specific rule that says what should be done next. Most installers, myself included, will start by building the drop-pipe assembly and connecting it to the pump. Personally, I prefer to complete the outdoor work first. That way, if weather conditions become undesirable, the rest of the work is inside the basement of the home.

CONNECTING A DROP PIPE TO A SUBMERSIBLE PUMP

The task of connecting a drop pipe to a submersible pump is simple. All this work is done above ground. The first step is screwing a brass male adapter that has a barb insert connection on the back of it into the pump. Threads on the male adapter have to be sealed with pipe thread sealant, and the fitting must be installed tightly. It is just a matter of turning the threaded fitting into the opening on the pump and then turning it clockwise until it is tight.

After the male adapter is installed, the next step is connecting the drop pipe. In this case we are using PE pipe. As a matter of principle, I always make these connections by using two stainless steel clamps.

A torque arrestor needs to be installed, and this is the time to do it. Slide it up the drop pipe before the pipe is attached to the male adapter. Loosen the clamps that are on each end of the torque arrestor. Slide the rubber device up on the drop pipe. Do not expand or secure it at this time. Electrical wiring will be installed through it before the torque arrestor is secured in place.

Now you can connect the piping to the pump. To do this, slide two stainless steel clamps over the end of the pipe. Push them along the pipe several inches to keep them out of the way. The next step is to insert the barb fitting on the male adapter into the end of the pipe. If the temperature is cold, it may be difficult to get the fitting into the pipe. Use a heat gun to warm the last few inches of the pipe. Don't get it too hot. PE pipe will melt, and you don't want that.

Once the barb is fully inserted into the pipe, you can slide the clamps down into place and tighten them. Make sure that the clamps compress the pipe against the barbed fitting. If you overtighten the clamps they will strip and have to be replaced. I use a torque wrench to prevent this. The clamps do need to be tight, but you don't want the worm drive in the clamp to give out.

Now that you have the pipe connected to the pump you should tie the end of a nylon safety rope to the pump. This rope will save the day later if you drop the pump and piping in the well when installing it or if the connection between the pipe and the pump fails. Not everyone installs a safety rope, but they should.

WIRING THE PUMP

When you are connecting wiring to the pump, be sure to follow the manufacturer's recommendations. Some pumps require two wires. Most of them require three wires. Since I am not a licensed electrician and I believe strongly in following the manufacturer's instructions for wiring installations, it is not my goal to tell you how to connect the wiring you are installing to the leads coming from the pump. However, I will discuss the rest of the process.

You should run appropriate wiring along the drop pipe. It will pass under the torque arrestor as it heads to the pump connection. Once the connection to the pump is made, you are ready to size and secure the torque arrestor. To do this, tighten the clamp on the torque arrestor that is closest to the pump. When this is done you can push down on the top of the rubber torque arrestor. Doing this will expand the device. It should be expanded to a point that allows it to fit freely down the well casing with minimal clearance on both sides.

A torque arrestor is installed to absorb jerks and vibrations created by the pump when it is cycling. This keeps the pump, wiring, and piping from bouncing into the well casing, which could damage the materials. The next step is extending the wiring up the length of the pipe. You will need electrical tape and torque stops to do this.

Slide some torque stops down the drop pipe. These devices are designed to allow wiring to pass through them. Torque stops are installed at regular intervals—spacing them about 10 feet apart is normally adequate. When you install torque stops you are adding another element of protection to keep the electrical wiring from rubbing against the well casing and chafing the electrical insulation.

Go ahead and run your wiring up the drop pipe. Leave a good amount running past the end of the pipe. When installed, the pipe will terminate at the pitless adapter, but the wiring must go to the top of the wellhead with sufficient length that it can be connected to wiring coming in from the trench. Use electrical tape to secure the wiring to the drop pipe between torque stops. This creates a professional installation. You are almost ready to connect the drop pipe to the pitless adapter.

CONNECTING THE DROP PIPE TO THE PITLESS ADAPTER

Before connecting the drop pipe to the pitless adapter you must cut the drop pipe to an appropriate length. Normally the pipe is long enough to submerge the pump deep into the well water without getting too close to the bottom of the well. The pump should be kept at least 20 feet off the bottom of the well. Because of the extreme depth of some wells, it is common for pumps to be hung so that there is much more distance between them and the bottom of the well.

Make sure that you have plenty of water covering the pump to allow for changes in water content. It makes little sense to hang a pump 100 feet deep when you can hang it 200 feet deep.

When you review the well specifications, you will find the depth of the well, the static water level, and the recovery rate of the well. This information prepares you for the minimum depth at which to install the pump. Consider the lift rating of the pump and make sure it is rated to pump the required distance.

When you have determined a proper length for the drop pipe, cut the assembled section from the remaining roll of piping. Cut the safety rope so that you will have at least 10 feet of rope extending on the top of the well casing.

Wrap the safety rope around the well casing several times and tie it securely. Remember, this rope could be all that stands between you and a lost pump if something goes wrong during the installation. The next step is connecting the drop pipe to the piece that slides into the pitless adapter. This is done with a brass fitting and stainless steel clamps.

Now you are ready to lower the pump into the well. The pitless adapter slide will accept the threads of a steel pipe. Most plumbers use a well tee for this installation. A well tee is a section of pipe that is 8 or 10 feet long. It has male threads on each end. One end is attached to a tee fitting, with the tee installed in a bullhead position. In other words, the center outlet attaches to the long pipe. A section of steel piping extends out of each of the other ends of the tee. These sections are usually about a foot long. They form a handle, which prevents the tool from falling down the well casing.

Thread the open end of the long tee shaft into the pitless fitting that is on the pipe. You don't need pipe thread sealant, and the connection does not have to be completely tight. The pipe section will be removed when the pump is installed.

LOWERING THE PUMP

Double-check all your work to this point. Refer to Figure 9.1 if you have any questions. If the work meets your satisfaction, you can lower the pump into the well. When you begin to lower the pump, it is important to make sure that the pipe is being lowered straight into the well. Do not let it slide over the edge of the well casing. This can damage the wiring and possibly the pipe. When the pump is completely lowered, slide the pitless fitting into place. This creates a positive seal and provides the support needed for the well pipe and pump. Once the slide adapter is seated completely, unscrew the well tee and remove it. Now you are ready to make the electrical connection at the wellhead.

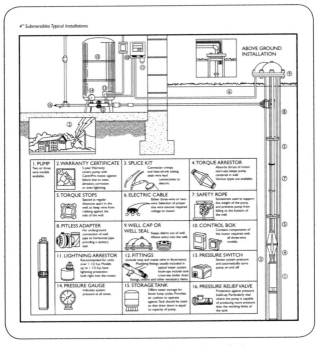

Figure 9.1 Typical Submersible Pump Installation
(Courtesy of Goulds Pumps)

CONNECTING WIRES AT THE WELLHEAD

Connecting wires at the wellhead requires the use of a splice kit. These are connectors that use a heat-shrinking means of making the wiring connections waterproof. The same connectors are used for any connections made along the drop pipe.

The ends of each wire to be connected are stripped of insulation. Once you have bare wires, slide them through the heat-shrinking sections and place them under the metallic connection points. When the copper wire is in the proper position, the connection points are squeezed hard with pliers to join the ends of two wires under each connection point.

Now you need a heat gun or a torch to shrink the collars on the splice kit. If you use a torch, be careful. Too much heat too close to the material will burn it and ruin the splice kit. A heat gun works great.

Move whatever heat source you are using around so that it is not concentrated on a particular portion of the material. As it is heated, the plastic will shrink and melt into place around the insulated wires to seal them from water infiltration. Now you can install the well cap and secure it. There will be a molded channel in the top that allows the wiring to be turned downward, toward the trench. This completes the outside work.

INSIDE THE FOUNDATION

You have some work to do inside the foundation. The first step is installing the pressure tank. After the tank is set in place and the air charge is tested, install the tank tee and associated devices. Make the connection between the water service and the tank. You can use the same instructions given for this under the information for jet pumps earlier in this chapter. When everything has been tested, seal the pipe sleeve and you are done.

10

BOOSTER PUMPS

Booster pumps are used to increase water supply when a plumbing system is not providing adequate service. These pumps are not common, but they are used when they are needed. They are sometimes used for residential homes, but they can be used with any plumbing system that needs to boost its water performance.

Don't expect a miracle from a booster pump. It is not an ultimate fix for an inadequate water supply, but it does make a noticeable difference. For example, a booster pump can provide an additional 30 psi of pressure when installed. This is significant.

Poor wells are not the only reason booster pumps may be needed. Even municipal water services can have inadequate pressure. How can this be? A damaged water service can be the culprit. If the pipe is crushed, it cannot deliver the quantity of water that it previously did. This would be a situation where a booster pump could be used to avoid having to dig up the water service.

GENERAL INFORMATION

Before going into the specifics of booster pumps, let's cover some general information. To make this simple, some key information is provided in the following bullet list.

▪ A booster pump can increase pressure in a system by 37 psi if no plumbing outlets are being used.

▪ For example, a water demand of 14 gpm can have up to 30 psi more pressure when a booster pump is used.

▪ Some booster pumps are able to perform suction lift, and others are not.

▪ Booster pumps are designed to be installed in a horizontal position. They should not be installed in a vertical position.

▪ Abrasive materials should not be allowed to enter a booster pump.

▪ Most booster pumps are equipped with cut-out protection to keep the pump from overheating or being damaged by the lack of water.

▪ A waterproof environment that is protected from freezing temperatures is required when a booster pump is installed.

▪ Booster pumps are not designed to work with systems in which water flow is less than 1.2 gpm.

▪ Booster pumps should not be installed in a location where drainage from the pump will damage a floor.

▪ Booster pumps can be used with municipal water supplies or private water sources.

▪ Booster pumps are sometimes used to maintain steady performance in water flow from a showerhead.

As you can see, there is a lot involved in the use of booster pumps; however, the information is not complicated. The concept behind booster pumps is pretty simple.

SIZING BOOSTER PUMPS

The sizing of booster pumps is done basically the same way that you would size a jet pump. If a pump is being sized for use with a municipal water supply, you will need to know what the existing incoming pressure is. Plumbing outlets should be open when you test the pressure. This will give you the dynamic suction pressure. If you do the test without plumbing being used, you will get static pressure, and that is not what you are after.

If you establish the dynamic suction pressure as 15 psi, you would use that number in your calculations. The actual number could be anything. The data in Table 10.1 is based on a dynamic suction pressure of 15 psi.

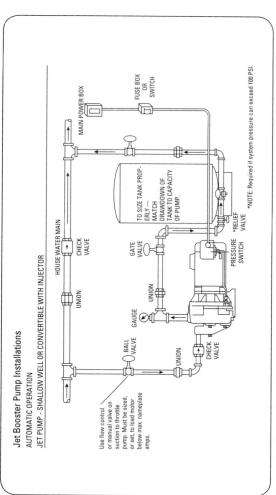

Jet Booster Pump Installations
AUTOMATIC OPERATION
JET PUMP - SHALLOW WELL OR CONVERTIBLE WITH INJECTOR

MAIN POWER BOX

FUSE BOX
OR
SWITCH

*NOTE: Required if system pressure can exceed 100 PSI.

HOUSE WATER MAIN

CHECK
VALVE

UNION

TO SIZE TANK PROP-
ERLY —
MATCH
DRAWDOWN OF
TANK TO CAPACITY
OF PUMP.

GATE
VALVE

UNION

*RELIEF
VALVE

PRESSURE
SWITCH

GAUGE

BALL
VALVE

UNION

CHECK
VALVE

Use flow control
or manual valve on
suction to throttle
pump. Must be sized,
or set to load motor
below max. nameplate
amps.

Figure 10.1 Jet Booster Pump Installations. Automatic Operation Jet Pump—Shallow Well or Convertible with Injector *(Courtesy of Goulds Pumps)*

Table 10.1 Sizing Information for a Booster Pump

(Courtesy of Goulds Pumps).

Flow Rate GPM	Pump Discharge Pressure (PSI)	incoming Dynamic Pressure (PSI)	Total Discharge Pressure (PSI)
11.5	20	15	35
11.3	30	15	45
11	40	15	55
7.7	50	15	65
4.8	60	15	75
0	83	15	98

INSTALLATION DIAGRAMS

Figures 10.2 through 10.8 show basic piping arrangements for booster pumps. They supply good visual instruction on how proper installations are made.

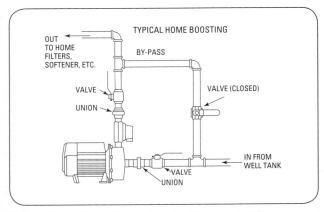

Figure 10.2 Typical Home Booster Pump Installation
(Courtesy of A Y McDonald)

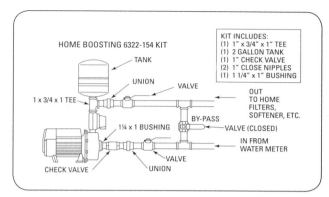

Figure 10.3 Home Booster Pump Installation with a Pressure Tank

(Courtesy of A Y McDonald)

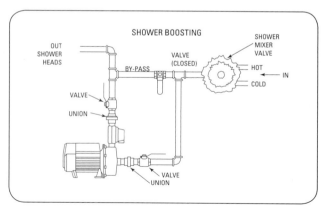

Figure 10.4 Example of Booster Pump Used for Boosting Shower Pressure

(Courtesy of A Y McDonald)

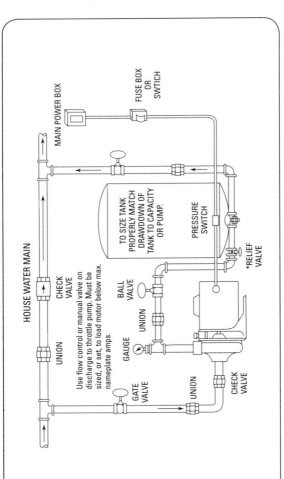

Figure 10.5 Piping Diagram for Automatic Centrifugal Booster Pump
(Courtesy of Goulds Pumps)

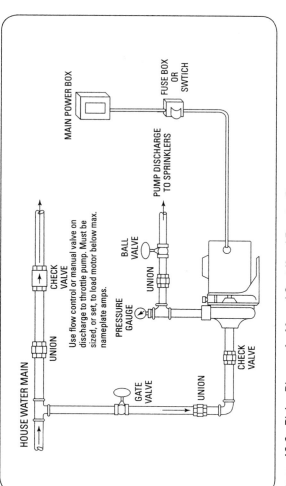

Figure 10.6 Piping Diagram for Manual Centrifugal Booster Pump
(Courtesy of Goulds Pumps)

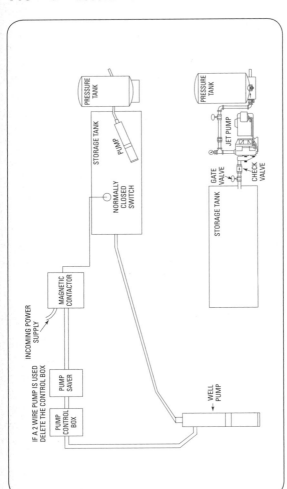

Figure 10.7 Illustration of Components for a Low-Yield Well with a Booster Pump
(Courtesy of Goulds Pumps)

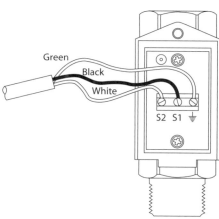

The 1507FS20 pump is supplied with the flow sensor uninstalled. This requires the flow sensor to be attached to the flow sensor cord from the pump.

- *Remove the flow sensor cover screw and remove cover.*
- *Remove cover cord nut and feed the cord through nut.*
- *Feed cord through black spacer.*
- *Remove inner core of orange grommet and discard.*
- *Feed cord through orange grommet and sensor cover.*
- *Install cover nut into cover leaving about 3" of wire inside.*
- *Connect the wires to the terminal block as shown below.*
- *White to S2, Black to S1 and Green to Ground ⊥*
- *Double check to make sure green wire is connected to ⊥*
- *Tighten terminal screws with a flat screw driver.*
- *Re-install the cover on the flow sensor.*

Figure 10.8 Wiring Instructions for a Booster Pump with a Sensor Cord

(Courtesy of A Y McDonald)

There is really no mystery to installing booster pumps. This chapter has supplied you with the basics. The information here will prepare you to research your specific needs. We are now ready to move into the water quality section of this book.

11

WATER QUALITY

Water quality is a serious topic. It is a concern for everyone. People who obtain their drinking water from wells should be especially knowledgeable about the potential risks that their water will become contaminated.

Well water can contain many naturally occurring elements that sound scary. Do you want to drink water that has arsenic in it? Arsenic is a natural element that shows up in some well water. As long as the volume is low enough, there is no real risk. It sounds like poison, and it is a potential poison, but in trace amounts it is not considered to be harmful.

Protecting wells from water contamination begins with choosing a location for the well. How surrounding grading is done to the land can also affect the potential risk of contamination. Well casings and grouting come into play when protecting a water source.

Water treatment systems are often installed on properties that are served by well water. These systems can simply treat hard water or control excess acid in water. There are even water treatment systems that can convert seawater into drinking water using reverse osmosis. The simplest form of water treatment is an in-line filter that traps sediment or provides charcoal filtration of the water. There are many options for dealing with certain water-related problems. How the end user of a water system deals with water quality is often a personal decision.

All new wells are required to be bleached after being installed. Once this cleaning process is completed, a water sample is taken. It is sent to a laboratory for testing that will deliver precise results of what the well water contains and what the volume of each element is. Once this is in hand, the well can be determined safe or unsafe.

It is possible for water conditions to change over time. A well that tests clean when it is installed can be contaminated later. Routine tests are a good idea, but they are not required.

Some components that affect water quality can be detected with simple observation. There are components that might be suspected after a visual examination of the water. Other samples are discovered through taste or smell. It is good for end users to be aware of these options for monitoring water quality.

Human behavior around a well can compromise water quality. The use of pesticides is an example of human activity that could contaminate a well. Ultimately, the quality of drinking water that is consumed can have major health effects. This chapter outlines a good deal of information to prepare professionals and consumers in the process of maintaining high water quality.

NOTICEABLE PROBLEMS

Sometimes there are noticeable problems associated with domestic water. These problems can be simple and annoying, but they can also indicate a more serious concern about the quality of the potable water being made available. Major issues, such as contamination with bacteria, heavy metals, nitrates, radon, and most chemicals, can be detected only with professional laboratory tests. Tables 11.1, 11.2, and 11.3 give you an idea of the types of problems that can be discovered without lab testing.

Table 11.1 Visible Examination of Potable Water

Condition	Cause
Scale or scum buildup	Calcium or magnesium salts in water
Cloudy water that does not clear	Dirt, clay salts, silt, or rust in water
Green stains on fixtures	High acidic content in water
Brownish-red stains on fixtures	Dissolved iron in water
Cloudy water that clears after standing	Possible air leak in pump, piping, or filter

Table 11.2 Taste Test of Potable Water

Condition	Cause
Salty taste	High sodium content in water
Soapy taste	Dissolved alkaline minerals in water
Metallic taste	High acid or iron content in water
Chemical taste	Possible chemicals in water

Table 11.3 Smell Test of Potable Water

Condition	Cause
Rotten egg smell	Dissolved hydrogen sulfide gas in water (sulfur)
Detergent smell with foamy water	Septic system could be leaching into water source
Gas or oil smell	Potential seepage from an underground tank entering water source
Musty smell	Decaying organic matter, such as leaves, in water source
Chlorine smell	Excessive chlorination of water

NATURALLY OCCURRING POLLUTANTS

Some sources of potable water contamination are the result of naturally occurring pollutants. This can occur in both shallow and deep wells. The five most common naturally occurring pollutants are as follows:

■ Microorganisms
■ Radionuclides
■ Nitrates and nitrites
■ Heavy metals
■ Fluoride

MICROORGANISMS

Microorganisms can include bacteria, viruses, and parasites. These conditions are detectable only with laboratory testing. Wells that are at the most risk for these types of pollutants are shallow wells, where the water is close to the ground surface.

If the grading around a well allows surface water to collect around the well, there is added risk. Heavy rains can wash pollutants into the water source. Fecal matter from livestock or wildlife can contribute greatly to water contamination if it is washed toward a well. Proper grading around a well can go a long way in preventing this type of contamination.

RADIONUCLIDES

Radionuclides are radioactive elements. Uranium and radium are examples of these types of elements, which are found in groundwater and underlying rock. Radon is a gas that people have become more aware of because it can pose a serious health risk. It is generated by the breakdown of uranium in the soil. It is believed that radon is a contributing factor in some cases of lung cancer.

NITRATES AND NITRITES

When nitrogen compounds break down in soils, they create nitrates and nitrites. A more common source of these pollutants is human activities, but the pollutants do occur naturally. The contaminants are delivered via flowing groundwater, and they pose a particular threat to infants who consume water containing them.

HEAVY METALS

Heavy metals can be found in soil and underground rocks. The metals can include arsenic, cadmium, chromium, lead, and selenium. It is rare for these pollutants to exist in dangerous levels in well water.

FLUORIDE

Fluoride is considered a beneficial water additive for dental health. However, excessive amounts can cause damage to bone tissue. Some regions have high concentrations of fluoride.

HUMAN ACTIVITY

Human activity can account for numerous types of water contamination. Some of this activity is necessary, but there are precautions that can be taken to reduce the associated risks. Examples of such activity are as follows:

- Concentrated animal feeding operations
- Heavy metals
- Fertilizers
- Pesticides
- Industrial products
- Industrial wastes
- Household waste
- Lead
- Copper
- Water treatment chemicals

This is a long list. Any activity near a water source that involves any of these elements has the potential to contaminate the water source. Proper use and management of these activities is the key to maintaining a safe drinking water supply. Table 11.4 lists some potential problems and the items to test for if they are encountered.

Table 11.4 Potential Problems and What to Test for Them

Condition	What to Test For
Gastrointestinal illness	Coliform bacteria
Lead contents	pH, lead, copper

(Continued)

Table 11.4 *(Continued)*

Condition	What to Test For
Radon in water or air	Radon
Local intensive agriculture	Nitrate, pesticides, coliform bacteria
Local mining operations	Metals, pH, corrosion
Local gas drilling	Chloride, sodium, barium, strontium
Local trash dump	Volatile organic compounds, total dissolved solids, pH, sulfate, chloride, metals
Buried fuel tanks nearby	Volatile organic compounds
Bad taste or smell	Hydrogen sulfide, corrosion, metals
Stained plumbing fixtures	Iron, copper, manganese
Salty taste	Chloride, total dissolved solids, sodium
Scaly residue	Hardness
Rapid wear on water treatment equipment	pH or corrosion
Water softener needed to treat water	Manganese or iron
Cloudy, frothy, or colored water	Color and detergents
Musty smell	Decaying organic material

Water quality is essential to healthy life. This section has provided insight into potential problems and solutions. It is far from comprehensive, but it sheds some light on things to consider. A lot of risk can be reduced with proper installation and grading around potable water sources. Common sense is an essential component in keeping water safe. Do your part.

12

TROUBLE- SHOOTING AND REPAIRS

Troubleshooting problems is a key to success for a service technician. During my 30-year career I have seen a lot of plumbers use a host of ways to find the sources of problems. The best technicians have all had something in common: They had a plan of action that they employed during the troubleshooting process.

A lot of people come upon a problem and don't know where to begin with a logical troubleshooting plan. They often play a hit-or-miss game until they figure out what is wrong. Others simply guess and hope. Then there are those who follow some source of information.

It is helpful to have data available to pull from when evaluating a problem. Working with a checklist can be very efficient. Experience with past problems is always helpful when troubleshooting. So how do you troubleshoot pump problems?

This chapter provides you with a wealth of troubleshooting data. Illustrations are included to show you the nature of a particular problem and the likely cause of it. These illustrations also suggest potential solutions to the problems.

Having specific information on the types of problems you will be working with is both advisable and important. However, it may not be enough. The outcome of a particular problem results from what you do and how you do it.

When you have solved a problem, it is a good idea to make notes on what you did. It is easy to assume that you will simply remember this information the next time you need it, but you might not. Gaining experience is a wonderful thing, but for it to do you much good you must learn from it and retain it.

Here we are dealing only with well systems. That does limit the possible problems and the probable solutions. What might surprise you is the amount of experience you will need with electrical meters when working with problem pumps. Many problems are related to the electrical system involved. Not all plumbers are good with meters. Some use them only to determine whether power is coming to a fixture, such as a water heater. In the case of pumps, the expertise needed with a meter is much more extensive.

It may seem odd, but there is often more electrical knowledge than plumbing experience necessary to solve pump problems. The last section of this chapter delves into specific uses of electrical meters to determine the root causes of problems with well systems.

Many of the figures and tables you will find here are detailed and self-explanatory and do not need a lot of text to enable you to understand the data. Thus, they are a quick way for you to get right to the heart of the process of troubleshooting potential problems.

GENERAL INFORMATION

An effective troubleshooting plan starts with a working knowledge of how a normal system should function and what it should look like. Figure 12.1 shows a typical installation for a submersible pump.

Figure 12.2 shows ratings for motor cooling, temperatures, flow rates, and timing, as well as explaining the cooling and lubrication of pumps. There is also a chart containing flow rates for motor cooling. This general information can be useful as a base point when troubleshooting a pump problem.

RULE OF THUMB

1. *Use same size or larger pipe as discharge on pump.*
2. *Always use a check valve for every 200 ft. of vertical pipe.*

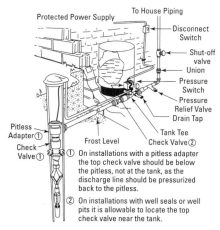

1. *On installations with a pitless adapter, the top check valve should be below the pitless, not at the tank, as the discharge line should be pressurized back to the pitless.*
2. *On installations with well seals or well pits, it is allowable to locate the top check valve near the tank.*

 CAUTION

All electrical equipment must be connected to supply ground. Follow applicable code requirements.

Figure 12.1 Typical Installation of a Two-Wire Submersible Pump

(Courtesy of Goulds Pumps)

MOTOR COOLING, TEMPERATURE, AND TIME RATINGS

All 4 inch CentriPro motors may be operated continuously in water up to 86° F. Optimum service life will be attained by maintaining a minimum flow rate past the motor of .25 feet per second. Use a Flow Sleeve if velocity is below the .25'/sec, if the well is top feeding or when the pump is used in a large body of water or large tank.

Six (6) inch canned design motors from 5 – 40 HP will operate in water up to 95° F (35° C), without any de-rating of horsepower, with a minimum flow rate of .5 ft./sec. past the motor. 6" – 50 HP and all 8" – 10" motors can operate in 77° F (25° C) water with .5'/sec velocity past the motor.

One way to make a flow sleeve is to install a well seal above the pump discharge and slip a piece of casing over the pump and affix it to the well seal. Drill three holes at 120° intervals on the lower section of the casing and insert (3) screws and nuts through the casing, just touching the motor. Tighten the nuts out against the casing. Insure that the screws do not protrude out too far as you don't want them catching on well joints.

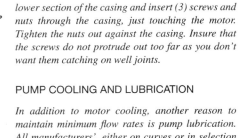

FLOW SLEEVE

PUMP COOLING AND LUBRICATION

In addition to motor cooling, another reason to maintain minimum flow rates is pump lubrication. All manufacturers', either on curves or in selection charts, show minimum flows. This insures that rotating pump parts are properly lubricated to prolong service life and reduce friction. A dead headed pump will super heat water very quickly, and hot water has no lubricity.

Figure 12.2   Motor Cooling, Temperature, Time Ratings, and Lubrication

(Courtesy of Goulds Pumps)

MINIMUM FLOW RATES FOR PROPER MOTOR COOLING

Well or Sleeve Diameter (inches)	3.75" Dia. 4" CP or FE Motor .25'/ sec.	CP = 5.5" Dia. 6" CP Motor .5'/ sec.	FE = 5.38" Dia. 6" FE Motor .5'/ sec.	CP = 7.52" Dia. 8" CP Motor .5'/ sec.
	GPM Required			
4	1.2	–	–	–
5	7	–	–	–
6	13	7	9	–
7	20	23	25	–
8	30	41	45	9
10	50	85	90	53
12	80	139	140	107
14	110	198	200	170
16	150	276	280	313

Multiply gpm by .2271 for m^3/Hr.
Multiply gpm by 3.785 for l/min.
(Courtesy of Goulds Pumps)

Suction lift is a source of potential problems. To determine satisfactory lift ability you will need a vacuum gauge. Figures 12.3 and 12.4 detail the use of this type of gauge.

A vacuum gauge indicates total suction lift (vertical lift + friction loss = total lift) in inches of mercury. 1" on the gauge = 1.13 ft. of total suction lift (based on pump located at sea level).

 ## RULE OF THUMB

Practical suction lift at sea level is 25 ft. Deduct 1 ft. of suction lift for each 1,000 ft. of elevation above sea level.

SHALLOW WELL SYSTEM

Install vacuum gauge in shallow well adapter. See opposite page. When pump is running, the gauge will show no vacuum if the end of suction pipe is not submerged or there is a suction leak. If the gauge shows a very high vacuum (22 inches or more), this indicates that the end of suction pipe is buried in mud, the foot valve or check valve is stuck closed or the suction lift exceeds capability of pump.

 ## High Vacuum (22 inches or more)

- *Suction pipe end buried in mud*
- *Foot valve or check valve stuck closed*
- *Suction lift exceeds capability of the pump*

 ## Low Vacuum (or 0 vacuum)

- *Suction pipe not submerged*
- *Suction leak*

Figure 12.3 Checking Suction Lift

(Courtesy of Goulds Pumps)

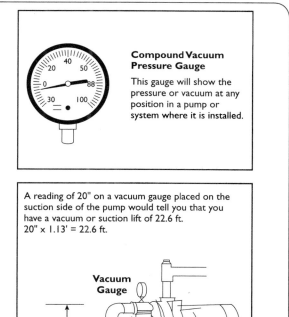

Compound Vacuum Pressure Gauge

This gauge will show the pressure or vacuum at any position in a pump or system where it is installed.

A reading of 20" on a vacuum gauge placed on the suction side of the pump would tell you that you have a vacuum or suction lift of 22.6 ft.
20" × 1.13' = 22.6 ft.

Vacuum Gauge

22.6' Vertical Lift Plus Friction

Figure 12.4 Establishing Suction Lift
(Courtesy of Goulds Pumps)

Pump rotation is a critical part of pump performance. If a pump is rotating in the wrong direction for an extended time, the pump and motor can be damaged. See Figure 12.5 for rotation details.

Correct rotation is a must on all 3Ø installations. Rotation can be checked by one of these three ways:

Visual 1

1. *Connect 3 motor leads to starter, run unit at open discharge.*
2. *Switch any 2 leads and again run unit at open discharge.*
3. *Largest quantity of water indicates correct rotation.*

Visual 2

Remove water end from meter. Run motor and observe rotation

Pressure

1. *Connect 3 motor leads to starter. Run unit against closed discharge, take maximum pressure reading.*
2. *Switch any 2 leads and again run unit against closed discharge. Take maximum pressure reading.*
3. *Highest pressure reading indicates correct rotation.*

 WARNING!

Prolonged reverse rotation operation can cause pump/motor damage.

Figure 12.5 Rotation Rules
(Courtesy of Goulds Pumps)

Pressure tanks are important components of normal well systems. See the chart for overall data on tank volumes. You can check the pressure of a tank by using the instructions presented below.

Tank Volumes

Model No.	Total Volume (Gals.)	Drawdown in Gals. at System Operating Pressure Range of			Max. Drawdown Vol. (Gals.)
		18/40 PSIG	28/50 PSIG	38/60 PSIG	
V6P	2.0	0.8	0.7	0.6	1.2
V15P	4.5	1.8	1.5	1.3	2.7
V25P	8.2	3.3	2.8	2.4	4.5
V45P	13.9	5.6	4.7	4.1	8.4
V45B	13.9	5.6	4.7	4.1	8.4
V45	13.9	5.6	4.7	4.1	8.4
V60B	19.9	8.0	6.8	5.8	12.1
V60	19.9	8.0	6.8	5.8	12.1
V80	25.9	10.4	8.8	7.6	13.9
V80EX	25.9	10.4	8.8	7.6	13.9
V100	31.8	12.8	10.8	9.4	13.8
V100S	31.8	12.8	10.8	9.4	13.8
V140B	45.2	18.2	15.4	13.3	27.3
V140	45.2	18.2	15.4	13.3	27.3
V200B	65.1	26.2	22.1	19.2	39.3
V200	65.1	26.2	22.1	19.2	39.3
V250	83.5	33.6	28.4	25.6	50.8
V260	84.9	34.1	28.9	25.0	44.7
V350	115.9	46.6	39.4	34.1	70.5

1 Drawdown based on a 22 psi differential and Boyle's Law. Temperature, elevation and pressure can all affect drawdown volume.

RULE OF THUMB

*Tank must be sized to **allow a minimum run time per cycle** as*
follows:
  $1/3$ – $1½$ HP = 1 minute run time
  2 HP & larger = 2 minute run time
(Courtesy of Goulds Pumps)

Procedure for Checking Tank Pressure

1. *To check: Shut off power supply and drain system to "0"*
   pressure.
2. *Air pre-charge in tank should be 2 psi less than the cut-in*
   pressure of the pressure switch.
Example: If pressure switch setting is 30–50 psi, tank should be
pre-charged with 28 lbs. air.

3. *If water at valve, replace tank.*

 RULE OF THUMB

Improper tank sizing may cause motor damage.
  ½ to 1½ HP pumps – Tank draw down should be equal to
    the pump capacity in GPM or greater.
  Example: ¾ HP pump; capacity 12 GPM; pressure switch
    setting 30/50 PSI; correct tank – V140.
  2 HP and larger pumps – tank drawdown should be double
    the pump capacity in GPM.
  Example: 3 HP pump; capacity 30 GPM; pressure switch
    setting 40/60 PSI; correct tank selection 2 – V350 tanks.
(Courtesy of Goulds Pumps)

It might be necessary to adjust the pressure control valves when
working with well systems. This is done either when the pump is first
started or under maximum flow conditions. Basically, you turn the adjustment to the left to reduce pressure and to the right to increase pressure.

Adjusting Pressure Control Valves

When pump is first started or under maximum flow condition, pressure control should be immediately adjusted to the pressure corresponding to H.P. and jet assembly used. See rating tables in catalog for proper pressure setting.

1. Turn left to reduce pressure.
2. Turn right to increase pressure.

 RULE OF THUMB

If pressure control valve is set too high, the air volume control will not function.

If pressure control valve is set too low, the pump may not shut off.

To Adjust Pressure Control Valve:

1. Close pressure control valve.
2. Open faucet in house.
3. Turn pump on.
4. As pump picks up its prime, the pressure will begin to rise on the gauge.
5. Turn adjusting screw to set pressure control valve to pressure recommended in catalog.

(Courtesy of Goulds Pumps)

PROBLEMS AND SOLUTIONS

Problems and solutions are what you will be working with as you trouble-shoot well systems. Collected here are a number of quick-check guides for you to use based on the type of problem you are dealing with. The illustrations present a type of problem and potential solutions for the problem. Using this information can save you a lot of time and frustration.

Let's say you have a pump that starts and builds pressure up to 40 psi without the switch cutting out. There are three likely causes for this problem. An associated problem can be a switch that is making noise. Table 12.1 outlines troubleshooting and repair procedures for this type of problem.

What do you do when a pump does not deliver 40 psi of tank pressure? See Table 12.2 for information on this type of problem.

Table 12.1 Pump Develops 40 psi Without the Switch Cutting Out

Pump Runs But ...	
Pump develops 40 lbs. pressure, but switch does not cut out ...	
Problem	**Recommended Action**
1. Pressure switch incorrectly set.	See Switch Adjustment.
2. Tubing or fittings between switch and pump plugged.	Remove switch tubing and/or all fittings and clean.
3. Faulty switch or corroded contact points.	Replace if necessary.
Switch Chatter ...	
Problem	**Recommended Action**
1. Caused by pressure differential between switch and tank. Equivalent feet of pipe should be less than 4' to prevent chatter. Friction loss of fittings can add many feet of equivalent pipe, ex. a ¾" - 90° elbow = 2' of pipe; 1" 90 = 2.7". See TTECHWP Tech Manusl for pipe fitting equivalents.	Move pressure switch to tank cross tee or mount in a discharge tee near pump.
2. High volume flows can cause switch chatter	Contact switch supplier (not pump mfg) for a pressure pulsation plug they have very small holes which can easily plug with dirt and sand - use only if absolutely nothing else works and water is clean.

(Courtesy of Goulds Pumps)

Table 12.2 Pump Is Not Developing 40 psi of Tank Pressure

Pumps water, but does not develop 40 lbs, tank pressure …	
Problem	**Recommended Action**
1. Leaks in well piping or discharge pipe.	Pressurize piping system and inspect.
2. Jet or screen on foot valve partially plugged.	Clean if necessary.
3. Improper pressure control valve setting (deep well only).	See Pump IOM
4. Suction lift too high for shallow well system. a. Jet set too deep for deep well system.	Use vacuum gauge on shallow well systems Vacuum should not exceed 22 inches at sea level. On deep well system check ratings tables in catalog for maximum jet depth.
5. Faulty air charger.	Disconnect the tubing and plug the hole. If this corrects the trouble, the air control must be replaced.
6. Worn impeller hub and/or guide vane bore.	Replace if necessary. Clearance should not exceed .012 on a side or .025 diametrically.
7. Overpumping the well.	Throttle a valve on the pump suction – do not exceed 22" Hg.

(Courtesy of Goulds Pumps)

The next case involves a pump that runs too frequently, which can wear it out. Notice in Table 12.3 that there are eight possible causes for a pump running too often. Your attention should be focused on the pressure tank, which is where you will most likely find the cause of your problem.

Another problem is a pump that runs but does not deliver much, if any, water. This can be due to anything from the pump losing its prime to a leak in a suction line. You have six considerations to evaluate, as outlined in Table 12.4.

Table 12.3 Pump Runs Too Often

Pump starts and stops too often...	
Problem	**Recommended Action**
1. Leaks in piping system.	Pressurize piping sstem and inspect. Repair or replace.
2. Faulty pressure switch.	Check contact points. Adjust or replace switch.
3. Waterlogged galvanized tank, faulty air control.	Pumps using Brady control: Test by holding your ear on air control. If control is operating, air can be heard passing from control into tank when pump stops. If no air movement is heard, air control should be replaced.
4. Leaking tank or air valve.	Use soapy water to find leaks. Repair or replace.
5. Not enough suction lift on shallow well system - water flows into pump (flooded suction).	Throttle suction line with partially closed valve.
6. Insufficient vacuum or vacuum does not exist for long enough time to operate air control.	Pump requires minimum 3" vacuum for 15 seconds.
7. Improper air change in captive air tank.	See tank checkout.
8. Tank too small for pump. for pump	Replace with proper size storage tank.

(Courtesy of Goulds Pumps)

Table 12.4 Pump Runs without Delivering Much, if Any, Water (Part A)

Pump Runs But ...	
Little or no water delivered	
Problem	**Recommended Action**
1. Pump or pipes not completely Primed.	Fill pump completely with water through priming opening (reprime pump). **a. Deep Well** system Control valve must be set properly or system will not pump. See **Pressure Control Valves**.
2. Foot valve or end of suction pipe either not submerged or buried. Foot valve in well or line check valve stuck colsed.	a. **Shallow Well system** Install vacuum gauge See **Checking Suction Lift**. **b. Deep Well** system Physically check well conditions. Replace foot valve if necessary. (Very high vacuum, 22 inches or more see **Checking Suction Lift**.
3. Leaks on suction side of pump (**Very common problem**.)	Pressurize system and inspect.

(Continued)

Table 12.4 (Continued)

Pump Runs But...	
Problem	**Reconended Action**
4. Jet assembly plugged.	A. **Shallow Well system** Clean if necessary (Insert wire through $^1/_2$" plug in shalkow well adapter.) b. Deep Well system Pull jet assembly and clean.
5. Punctured diaphragm in air control. Galvanized tanks	Disconnect the tubing and plug the connection in pump. If this corrects the trouble, the air control must be replaced.
6. Original installation, incorrect nozzle or diffuser combination.	Check rating in product catalog.

(Courtesy of Goulds Pumps)

Sometimes a pump simply will not run. This can be as fundamental as a tripped circuit breaker or as major as a bad motor. See Table 12.5 for advice on handling this type of a problem.

Table 12.5 Pump Will Not Run

Pumjp Will Not Run ...	
Probable	**Recommended Action**
1. Blown fuse or power turned off	Replace fuse-dose all switches.
2. Broken or loose wiring connection.	Examine all eiring and repair any bad connections.
3. Motor overload protection contacts open. a. Improper voltage. b. Pump bound mechanically-will not turn freely.	Overload contacts will close automatically in a short time. See volt Ammeter Remove motor end cap, turn motor shaft by hand. Unit should rotate freely.
4. Pressure switch faulty or out of adjustment.	Adjust or replace switch.
5. Tubing or fittings on pressure switch plugged.	Remove switch tubing and/or all fittings and clean.
6. Faulty motor.	See Jet pump ohmmter checks.

(Courtesy of Goulds Pumps)

We have now covered the basics of general plumbing problems with well systems. However, we are not finished yet. We have completed the typical piping and plumbing troubleshooting, but the electrical side of the process is still to come—and it is extensive.

ELECTRICAL INSTRUCTIONS

Electrical meters are key tools when it comes to troubleshooting pumps and well systems. You will find yourself using an Amprobe, which is a combination ammeter and voltmeter. You will need an ohmmeter to measure resistance in ohms. A Megger meter is used to measure insulation resistance to ground.

Amprobe Meter

The Amprobe is a multi-range, combination ammeter and voltmeter.

Voltmeter Scales:	150 Volts	600 Volts
Ammeter Scales:	5 Amps	40 Amps
	15 Amps	100 Amps

1. *When used as an ammeter, the tongs are placed around the wire being measured with the rotary scale on the **100 amp range**. Then rotate the scale back to the smaller ranges until an exact reading is indicated.*
2. *When used as a voltmeter, the two leads are clipped into the bottom of the instrument with the rotary scale on the 600 volt range. If the reading is less than 150 volts, rotate the scale to the 150 volt range to get a more exact reading.*

(Courtesy of Goulds Pumps)

Ohmmeter

The Ohmmeter is used for measuring the electrical resistance of a wire circuit. The unit of measurement is called an Ohm.

1. *The knob at the bottom of the Ohmmeter is adjustable through six ranges:*

RX_1	$= R \times 1$
RX_{10}	$= R \times 10$
RX_{100}	$= R \times 100$
RX_{1000}	$= R \times 1,000$
RX_{10K}	$= R \times 10,000$
RX_{100K}	$= R \times 100,000$

If your ohmmeter is digital readout type, refer to the instructions that came with it.

2. *The round center knob is for the purpose of adjusting the instrument to zero (0) after clipping the two ohmmeter leads together.* **This must be done every time the range selection is changed**.

 CAUTION

Use Ohmmeter only with power off.

(Courtesy of Goulds Pumps)

Megger Meter

This instrument is used to measure insulation resistance to ground. It consists of a crank-turned magneto, on the side of the case, and will give very close readings calibrated directly in ohms. It is cranked at a moderate rate of speed, approximately 120 rpm, until the pointer reaches a steady deflection.

1. *If the ohm value is normal, the motor windings are not grounded and the cable insulation is not damaged.*
2. *If the ohm value is below normal, either the windings are grounded or the cable insulation is damaged. Check the cable at the well seal as the insulation is sometimes damaged by being pinched.*

(Courtesy of Goulds Pumps)

The following illustrations give you a host of troubleshooting information about electrical matters.

Testing a Voltage Relay

WARNING!

Open master breaker and disconnect all leads from starter to avoid damage to meter or electric shock hazard. Connect the ohmmeter leads as shown above.

COIL WITH OHMMETER

1. *Set R × 1000.*
2. *Connect leads as shown.*
3. *Reading: Should register some value, Approx. 200–1000 ohms.*

WHAT IT MEANS

Infinity reading indicates coil is open. Zero reading indicates coil is shorted. In either case, the coil should be replaced.

A reading of 200–1000 ohms indicates coil is ok.

VOLTAGE RELAY

Control Boxes (CentriPro or F.E.)
Checking Relay with Ohmmeter

A. Voltage Relay Tests

Step 1. Coil Test
   1. Meter setting: R × 1,000.
   2. Connections: #2 & #5.
   3. Correct meter readings:
For 115 Volt Boxes:
   .7 – 1.8 (700 to 1,800 ohms).
For 230 Volt Boxes
   4.5 – 7.0 (4,500 to 7,000 ohms).
Step 2. Contact Test
   1. Meter setting: R × 1.
   2. Connections: #1 & #2.
   3. Correct meter reading: Zero for all models.

B. F.E. Blue Relay—Solid State $1/3$ – 1 HP QD Control Boxes

Used from 1994 until present time:
Step 1. Triac Test
   1. Meter setting: R × 1,000.
   2. Connections: Cap and B terminal.
   3. Correct meter reading: Infinity for all models.
Step 2. Coil Test
   1. Meter setting: R × 1.
   2. Connections: L1 and B.
   3. Correct meter reading: Zero ohms for all models.

(Courtesy of Goulds Pumps)

Checkout Procedure for Magnetic and Other Contactors

Contactor Coil Test

(Disconnect lead from one side of coil)
1. *Meter setting: R × 100*
2. *Connections: Coil terminals*
3. *Correct meter reading: 180 to 1,400 ohms*

Contactor Contact Test

1. *Meter Setting: R × 1*
2. *Connections: L1 & T1 or L2 & T2*
3. *Manually close contacts*
4. *Correct meter reading: Zero ohms*

(Courtesy of Goulds Pumps)

An ohmmeter is used to check for overloads. Keep reading for instructions for testing a pump that has a minimum of 1.5 horsepower.

Checking for Overloading on a Control Box for a Submersible Pump with a Minimum of 1.5 Horsepower

For 1½ HP (and Larger) Control Box

1. *Set Ohmmeter at "R × 1"*
2. *Connect the Ohmmeter leads to Terminal #1 and #3 on each Overload Protector.*
3. *Reading should be not more than 0.5 Ohms maximum on the scale.*

(Courtesy of Goulds Pumps)

Ohmmeters are also used to check capacitors and fuses.

Checking a Capacitor

  CAUTION

*Discharge the capacitor before making
this check. (A screwdriver can be used to
make contact between capacitor's posts.)*

1. *Disconnect leads to capacitor post.*
2. *Setting: R × 1,000*
3. *Connect ohmmeter leads to capacitor posts.*
4. *Reading: Pointer should swing toward zero, then back toward
   infinity.*

(Courtesy of Goulds Pumps)

Testing Fuses

1. *Set R × 1.*
2. *Connect leads as shown.*
3. *Reading: Should register zero.*

WHAT IT MEANS –

*Zero reading indicates fuse OK. Infinity (∞) reading indicates bad
fuse.*

(Courtesy of Goulds Pumps)

Voltage is always a potential consideration in the troubleshooting of
some pumps.

Checking Voltage with Q.D. Type Control Box

To Check Voltage with "Q.D." Type Control Box

1. *Remove cover to break all motor connections.*

 CAUTION

   L_1 and L_2 are still connected to power.

2. *To check VOLTAGE: Use voltmeter on L1 and L2 as shown.*
3. *When checking voltage, all other major electrical appliances (that could be in use at the same time) should be running.*
4. *If readings are not within the limits (see chart), call your power supplier.*

Voltage Limits		
	Measured Volts	
Nameplate ▼	**Min.**	**Max.**
115V 1Ø	105	125
208V 1Ø	188	228
230V 1Ø	210	250

(Courtesy of Goulds Pumps)

Checking Voltage at Fused Disconnect and Magnetic Starter

 WARNING!

Power is ON during voltage checking.

1. *To check voltage: Use voltmeter on L1, L2 and L3 in sequence. Check should be made at four locations.*
    Step 1 *Checking incoming power supply.*
    Step 2 *Checking fuses.*
    Step 3 *Checking contact points*
    Step 4 *Checking heaters.*
2. *When checking voltage, all other major electrical appliances (that could be in use at the same time) should be running.*
3. *If incoming power supply readings are not within the limits (see chart), call your power supplier.*

Voltage Limits		
	Measured Volts	
Name Plate ▼	**Minimum**	**Maximum**
208V 3Ø	188	228
230V 3Ø	207	253
460V 3Ø	414	506
575V 3Ø	518	632

NOTE: Phase to phase – full line voltage.
Phase to neutral – ½ full line voltage.
(depending on transformer connection)

(Courtesy of Goulds Pumps)

When you are testing amperage you need some basis to go on. Table 12.6 is an example of what you will need when you use your Amprobe to check amperage readings.

Table 12.6 Service Factor Amps

Service Factor Amps with QD ($^1/_2$–1 HP) or CSCR (1.5 HP & Larger) Control Boxes

4" 1Ø		CP 3-Wire			F.E. 3-Wire			CP 2-Wire	F.E. 2-Wire
HP	Volts	Yel	Black	Red	Yel	Black	Red	Black	Black
$^1/_2$	115	12.6	12.6	0	12.0	12.0	0	9.5	12.0
$^1/_2$		6.3	6.3	0	6.0	6.0	0	4.7	6.0
3/4		8.3	8.3	0	8.0	8.0	0	6.4	8.0
1		9.7	9.7	0	9.8	9.8	0	9.1	9.8
$1^1/_2$	230	11.1	11.0	1.3	11.5	11.0	1.3	11.0	13.1
2		12.2	11.7	2.6	13.2	11.9	2.6	N/A	
3		16.5	13.9	5.6	17.0	12.6	6.0		
5		27.0	22.0	10.0	27.5	19.1	10.8		

Service Factor Amps with Magnetic Contactor Control Boxes

6" 1Ø		CentriPro 3-Wire			Franklin Elec 3-Wire		
HP	Volts	Yel	Black	Red	Yel	Black	Black
5		27.5	N/A	N/A	27.5	17.4	10.5
7.5	230	41.0	N/A	N/A	42.1	40.5	5.4
10		58.0	N/A	N/A	51.0	47.5	8.9
15		85.0	N/A	N/A	75.0	62.5	16.9

(Courtesy of Goulds Pumps)

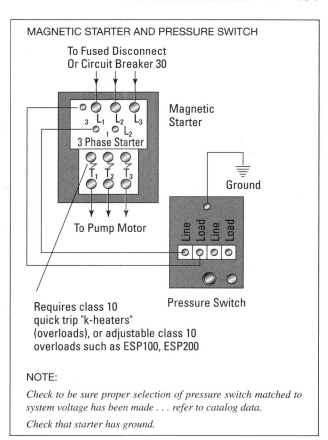

Figure 12.6 Typical Wiring Diagram for a Magnetic Starter and Pressure Switch

(Courtesy of Goulds Pumps)

TYPICAL WIRING DIAGRAMS

Figure 12.6 is an example of how a typical wiring diagram would look for a magnetic starter and pressure switch. Figures 12.7 and 12.8 provide overviews of normal wiring diagrams.

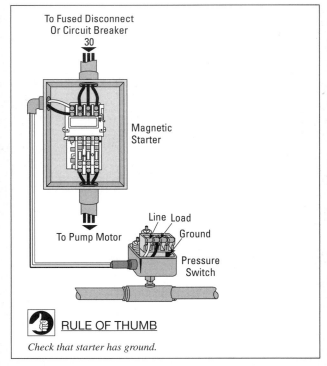

To Fused Disconnect
Or Circuit Breaker

30

Magnetic
Starter

To Pump Motor

Line Load
Ground

Pressure
Switch

RULE OF THUMB

Check that starter has ground.

Figure 12.7 Wiring Diagram between Circuit Breaker and Pressure Switch

(Courtesy of Goulds Pumps)

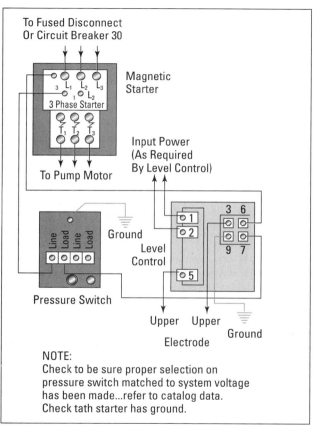

Figure 12.8 Magnetic Starter, Pressure Switch, and Liquid Level Control

(Courtesy of Goulds Pumps)

MORE ELECTRICAL TESTING

More electrical testing procedures are described here. The first test is checking electrical cable and splices.

Checking Electrical Cable and Splices

Checking Cable and Splice

1. *Submerge cable and splice in steel barrel of water with both ends out of water.*
2. *Set ohmmeter selector on R×100K and adjust needle to zero (0) by clipping ohmmeter leads together.*
3. *After adjusting ohmmeter, clip one ohmmeter lead to barrel and the other to each cable lead individually, as shown.*
4. *If the needle deflects to zero (0) on any of the cable leads, pull the splice up out of the water. If the needle falls back to (∞) (no reading) the leak is in the splice.*
5. *If leak is not in the splice, pull the cable out of the water slowly until needle falls back to (∞) (no reading). When the needle falls back, the leak is at that point.*
6. *If the cable or splice is bad, it should be repaired or replaced.*

(Courtesy of Goulds Pumps)

Sometimes the pump motor insulation resistance creates a problem. To check for this use Figure 12.9 and the chart that follows.

1. *Set the scale lever to R × 100K and adjust to 0.*

 CAUTION

   Open (turn off) master breaker and disconnect all leads from control box or pressure switch (Q-D type control, remove lid) to avoid damage to meter or electric shock hazard.

2. *Connect an ohmmeter lead to any one of the motor leads and the other to the metal drop pipe. If the drop pipe is plastic, connect the ohmmeter lead to the metal well casing or ground wire.*

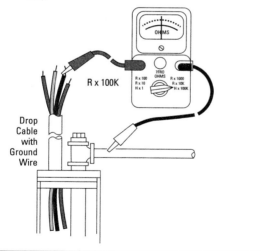

Figure 12.9 Checking Motor Insulation Resistance
(Courtesy of Goulds Pumps)

Normal Ohm and Megohm Values

NORMAL OHM AND MEGOHM VALUES (INSULATION
RESISTANCE) BETWEEN ALL LEADS AND GROUND

*Insulation resistance does not vary with rating. All motors of all
HP, voltage and phase rating have similar values of insulation
resistance.*

Condition of Motor and Leads	Ohms Value	Megohm Value
A new motor (without drop cable).	20,000,000 (or more)	20.0
A used motor which can be reinstalled in the well.	10,000,000 (or more)	10.0
New motor in the well	2,000,000 (or more)	2.0 (or more)
Motor in the well in good condition	500,000 – 2,000,000	0.5 – 2.0
Insulation damage, locate and repair	Less than 500,000	Less than .50

WHAT IT MEANS

1. *If the ohm value is normal, the motor windings are not
   grounded and the cable insulation is not damaged.*
2. *If the ohm value is below normal, either the windings are
   grounded or the cable insulation is damaged. Check the cable
   at the well seal as the insulation is sometimes damaged by
   being pinched.*

(Courtesy of Goulds Pumps)

There will be times when you will want to check the resistance of
motor windings. Figure 12.10 and the charts that follow give instructions
for doing this.

1. *Set the scale lever to R × 1 for values under 10 ohms. For values over 10 ohms, set the scale lever to R × 10. Zero balance the ohmmeter as described earlier.*

WARNING!

Open master breaker and disconnect all leads from starter to avoid damage to meter or electric shock hazard. Connect the ohmmeter leads as shown below.

2. *Connect the ohmmeter leads as shown below.*

CABLE RESISTANCE – COPPER

Size Cable	Paired wire
	Resistance (ohms per foot)
14	.0050
12	.0032
10	.0020
8	.0013
6	.0008
4	.0005
2	.0003
0	.0002
00	.00015
000	.00013
0000	.00010

See motor data pages for motor resistance ratings.

If aluminum cable is used the readings will be higher. Divide the ohm readings on this chart by 0.61 to determine the actual resistance of aluminum cable.

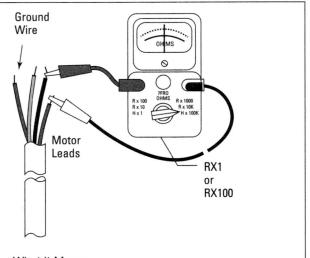

What it Means

1. *If all ohm values are normal, the motor windings are neither shorted nor open, and the cable colors are correct.*
2. *If any one ohm value is less than normal, the motor is shorted.*
3. *If any one ohm value is greater than normal, the winding or the cable is open or there is a poor cable joint or connection.*
4. *If some ohm values are greater than normal and some less, the leads are mixed.*

Figure 12.10 Checking Motor Winding Resistance
(Courtesy of Goulds Pumps)

Motor Resistance Ratings

Motor Resistance

1Ø Motors – Winding Resistance: Motor Only (Ohms)

	4" Motors		CentriPro		Franklin Electric	
Type	**HP**	**Volts**	**Winding Resistance**	**KVA Code**	**Winding Resistance**	**KVA Code**
2-Wire (PSC)	½	115	1.3–1.8	K	1.0–1.3	R
	½	230	4.5–5.2	K	4.2–5.2	R
	¾	230	3.0–4.8	J	3.0–3.6	N
	1	230	4.2–5.2	F	2.2–2.7	N
	1½	230	1.9–2.3	H	1.5–1.9	M

	4" Motors		CentriPro			Franklin Electric		
			Resistance		**KVA Code**	**Resistance**		**KVA Code**
Type	**HP**	**Volts**	**Main (B-Y.)**	**Start (R-Y)**		**Main (B-Y)**	**Start (R-Y)**	
3-Wire w/Q.D. Cap. Start	½	115	.9–1.6	5.7–7.0	N	1.0–1.3	4.1–5.1	M
	½		4.2–4.9	17.4–18.7	M	4.2–5.2	16.7–20.5	M
	¾		2.6–3.6	11.8–13	L	3.0–3.6	10.7–13.1	M
	1		2.2–3.2	11.3–12.3	L	2.2–2.7	9.9–12.1	L
3-Wire w/CSCR (CR) Control Box	1½	230	1.6–2.3	7.9–8.7	J	1.7–2.2	8.0–9.7	J
	2		1.6–2.2	10.8–12.0	G	1.8–2.3	5.8–7.2	G
	3		1.1–1.4	2.0–2.5	G	1.0–1.5	3.5–4.4	H
	5		.62–.76	1.36–1.66	E	.68–1.0	1.8–2.2	F

	6" Motors		CentriPro				Franklin Electric		
Type	**HP**	**Volts**	**Resistance**			**KVA Code**	**Resistance**		**KVA Code**
			R-Y	**B-Y**	**R-B**		**(B-Y)**	**(R-Y)**	
6° 1Ø	5	230	2.17	0.51	2.63	G	.55–.68	1.3–1.7	E
	7.5		1.40	0.4	1.77	F	.36–.50	.88–1.1	F
	10		1.05	0.316	1.31	E	.27–.33	.80–.99	E
	15		0.68	0.23	0.85	D	.17–.22	.68–.93	E

RULE OF THUMB

*Add resistance of drop cable when checking pump in well. See
    Cable Resistance.*

(Courtesy of Goulds Pumps)

The troubleshooting process can get complicated. With the help of
the kind of information provided here, the process becomes much less
mysterious. You now have plenty of data to get you off to a good start
when troubleshooting a well system. It never hurts to have your own cheat
sheets assembled from years of experience, so be sure to keep notes as
you solve problems.

A methodical approach is the most effective means of completing a
troubleshooting task. Don't bounce from one thing to another. Develop a
plan and work your plan. If you follow this procedure, the problems are
likely to be solved sooner.

Appendix

ADDITIONAL INFORMATION AND RESOURCES

WELL FAQ

Frequently Asked Questions

Where does the drinking water in my home come from?

The drinking water that is supplied to our homes comes from either surface water or ground water. Surface water is collected on the ground, in a stream, river, lake, reservoir, or ocean. Ground water is obtained by drilling wells and is located below the ground surface in pores and spaces within rocks. Public water systems usually provide treated water from surface and ground water for public use. Water treatment systems are either government or privately-held facilities that withdraw water from the source, treat it, and deliver it to our homes. For more information on public water systems, visit CDC's Healthy Water Public Water Systems page (http://www.cdc.gov/healthywater/drinking/public) A private well uses ground water as its water source. Owners of private wells and other individual water systems are responsible for ensuring that their water is safe from contaminants. For more information on private wells and individual water systems, visit CDC's Healthy Water Private Wells page (http://www.cdc.gov/healthywater/drinking/private/wells)

What are the main types of ground water wells?

According to the United States Environmental Protection Agency (EPA), there are three basic types of private drinking wells:

∎ Dug (http://www.epa.gov/safewater/privatewells/basic_dug.html)
∎ Drilled (http://www.epa.gov/safewater/privatewells/basic_drilled.html)
∎ Driven (http://www.epa.gov/safewater/privatewells/basic_driven.html)

Proper well construction and continued maintenance are keys to the safety of your water supply. It is important to know the type of well you have. You may be able to determine the type of well you have by looking at the outer casing and cover of the well.

As a private well owner, should I have my well tested?

Yes, as a private well owner, you are responsible for ensuring that you well water is safe to drink. The United States Environmental Protection Agency (EPA) is responsible for making sure that the public water supply within the United States is safe. However, the EPA does not monitor or treat private well drinking water. For information on testing your well water, visit Healthy Water's Well Testing (http://www.cdc.gov/healthy-water/drinking/private/wells/testing.html).

How do contaminants (germs and chemicals) get into my well water?

A private well uses ground water as its water source. There are many sources of contamination of ground water. Here is a list of the most common sources of contaminants:

∎ Naturally occurring chemicals and minerals (for example, arsenic, radon, uranium)
∎ Local land use practices (fertilizers, pesticides, livestock, animal feeding operations, biosolids application)
∎ Manufacturing processes
∎ Sewer overflows

■ Malfunctioning wastewater treatment systems (for example, nearby septic systems)

My well water has a funny smell or taste; should I worry about getting sick?

Any time you notice a significant change in your water quality, you should have it tested. A change in your water's taste, color, or smell is not necessarily a health concern. However, a change could be a sign of a serious contamination problem.

What germs and chemicals should I test for in my well?

Several water quality indicators (WQIs) and contaminants that should be tested for in your water are listed below. A WQI test is a test that measures the presence and amount of certain germs in water. In most cases, the presence of WQIs is not the cause of sickness; however, they are easy to test for and their presence may indicate the presence of sewage and other disease-causing germs from human and/or animal feces. For more information on these contaminants and WQIs, please see the Healthy Water Well Testing page (http://www.cdc.gov/healthywater/drinking/private/wells/testing.html).

Water Quality Indicators:

■ Total Coliforms
■ Fecal Coliforms / Escherichia coli (E. coli)
■ pH

Contaminants:

■ Nitrate
■ Volatile Organic Compounds (VOCs)

Other germs or harmful chemicals that you should test for will depend on where your well is located on your property, which state you live in, and whether you live in an urban or rural area. These tests could include testing for lead, arsenic, mercury, radium, atrazine, and other pesticides. You should check with your local health or environmental department to find out if any of these contaminants are a problem in your region. Please remember that if your test results say that there are germs or chemicals in your water, you should contact your local health or environmental department for help in interpreting the test, test your water more often, and receive guidance on how to respond to the contamination.

When should I have my well tested?

You should have your well tested once each year for total coliform bacteria, nitrates, total dissolved solids, and pH levels. If you suspect other contaminants, you should test for those as well. However, spend time identifying potential problems as these tests can be expensive. You should also have your well tested if:

▪ There are known problems with well water in your area
▪ You have experienced problems near your well (i.e., flooding, land disturbances, and nearby waste disposal sites)
▪ You replace or repair any part of your well system.
▪ You notice a change in water quality (i.e., taste, color, odor)

Who should test my well?

State and local health or environmental departments often test for nitrates, total coliforms, fecal coliforms, volatile organic compounds, and pH (see above). Health or environmental departments, or county governments should also have a list of the state-certified (licensed) laboratories in your area that test for a variety of Water Quality Indicators (WQIs) and contaminants.

For more information, visit one of the links below or contact your local health department or the EPA Safe Drinking Water Hotline at (800) 426-4791.

▪ Well Water Information Based on Where You Live (Environmental Protection Agency: http://water.epa.gov/drink/info/well/whereyoulive .cfm)
▪ State Certified Drinking Water Laboratories (Environmental Protection Agency: http://water.epa.gov/scitech/drinkingwater/labcert/ index.cfm)

WELL MAINTENANCE

Overview of Maintenance

Regular maintenance of your well is required to ensure the continued safety of your water and to monitor for the presence of any contaminants. The National Ground Water Association provides information to help you schedule a wellwater check up , or you can learn "How to Get Information on Wells Where You Live", below. If you still have questions, take a look at the Well Water FAQ.

According to the National Ground Water Association, here are some steps you can take to help protect your well:

- Wells should be checked and tested ANNUALLY for mechanical problems, cleanliness, and the presence of certain contaminants, such as coliform bacteria, nitrates/nitrites, and any other contaminants of local concern, (for example, arsenic and radon).
- Well water should be tested more than once a year if there are recurrent incidents of gastrointestinal illness among household members or visitors and/or a change in taste, odor, or appearance of the well water.
- All hazardous materials, such as paint, fertilizer, pesticides, and motor oil, should be kept far away from your well.
- When mixing chemicals, do not put the hose inside the mixing container, as this can siphon chemicals into a household's water system.
- Consult a professional contractor to verify that there is proper separation between your well, home, waste systems, and chemical storage facilities.
- Always check the well cover or well cap to ensure it is intact. The top of the well should be at least one foot above the ground.
- Once your well has reached its serviceable life (usually at least 20 years), have a licensed or certified water well driller and pump installer decommission the existing well and construct a new well. For more information visit "Finding a Contractor " (National Ground Water Association).

How to Get Information on Wells Where You Live

For more information, visit one of the links below or contact your local health department or the EPA Safe Drinking Water Hotline at (800) 426-4791.

■ Well Water Information Based on Where You Live (Environmental Protection Agency)
■ State Certified Drinking Water Laboratories (Environmental Protection Agency)

WELL TREATMENT

Treatment of Well Water

There are many different treatment options for the treatment of well waters. No single treatment type will protect against all problems. Many well owners use a home water treatment unit to:

■ Remove specific contaminants
■ Take extra precautions because a household member has a compromised immune system
■ Improve the taste of drinking water

Household water treatment systems are composed of two categories: point-of-use and point-of-entry. Point-of-entry systems are typically installed after the water meter and treat most of the water entering a residence. Point-of-use systems are systems that treat water in batches and deliver water to a tap, such as a kitchen or bathroom sink or an auxiliary faucet mounted next to a tap.

The most common types of household water treatment systems consist of:

Filtration Systems
A water filter is a device which removes impurities from water by means of a physical barrier, chemical, and/or biological process.
Water Softeners
A water softener is a device that reduces the hardness of the water. A water softener typically uses sodium or potassium ions

to replace calcium and magnesium ions, the ions that create "hardness."

Distillation Systems

Distillation is a process in which impure water is boiled and the steam is collected and condensed in a separate container, leaving many of the solid contaminants behind.

Disinfection

Disinfection is a physical or chemical process in which pathogenic microorganisms are deactivated or killed. Examples of chemical disinfectants are chlorine, chlorine dioxide, and ozone. Examples of physical disinfectants include ultraviolet light, electronic radiation, and heat.

In order to determine the best treatment option, contact a water well systems contractor.

For more information, visit one of the links below or contact your local health department or the EPA Safe Drinking Water Hotline at (800) 426-4791.

■ Well Water Information Based on Where You Live (Environmental Protection Agency)
■ State Certified Drinking Water Laboratories (Environmental Protection Agency)

For more information on personal household water treatment options, visit:

■ Drinking Water Treatment for Household Use (CDC)
■ Selecting a Household Water Treatment System (NSF International)
■ Water & Health Series: Filtration Facts   (Environmental Protection Agency)

WELL TESTING

Overview

The U.S. Environmental Protection Agency's (EPA) rules that protect public drinking water systems do not apply to individual water systems, such as privately owned wells. As an individual water system owner, it is up to you to make sure that your water is safe to drink.

What to Test for in Your Well

Several water quality indicators (WQIs) and contaminants that should be tested for in your water are listed below. A WQI test is a test that measures the presence and amount of certain germs in water. In most cases, the presence of WQIs is not the cause of sickness; however, they are easy to test for and their presence may indicate the presence of sewage and other disease-causing germs from human and/or animal feces. (Please see Water-related Diseases and Contaminants in Private Wells for a list of additional germs and chemicals in drinking water wells and the illnesses they cause.)

Examples of Water Quality Indicators:

Total Coliforms

Coliform bacteria are microbes found in the digestive systems of warm-blooded animals, in soil, on plants, and in surface water. These microbes typically do not make you sick; however, because microbes that do cause disease are hard to test for in the water, "total coliforms" are tested instead. If the total coliform count is high, then it is very possible that harmful germs like viruses, bacteria, and parasites might also be found in the water.

Fecal Coliforms / Escherichia coli (E. coli)

Fecal coliform bacteria are a specific kind of total coliform. The feces (or stool) and digestive systems of humans and warm-blooded animals contain millions of fecal coliforms. E. coli is part of the fecal coliform group and may be tested for by itself. Fecal coliforms and E. coli are usually harmless. However, a positive test may mean that feces and harmful germs have found their way into your water system. These harmful germs can cause diarrhea, dysentery, and hepatitis. It is important not to confuse the test for the common and usually harmless WQI E. coli with a test for the more dangerous germ E. coli O157:H7.

pH

The pH level tells you how acidic or basic your water is. The pH level of the water can change how your water looks and tastes. If the pH of your water is too low or too high, it could damage your pipes, cause heavy metals like lead to leak out of the pipes into the water, and eventually make you sick.

Examples of Contaminants:

Nitrate

Nitrate is naturally found in many types of food. However, high levels of nitrate in drinking water can make people sick. Nitrate in your well water can come from animal waste, private septic systems, wastewater, flooded sewers, polluted storm water runoff, fertilizers, agricultural runoff, and decaying plants. The presence of nitrate in well water also depends on the geology of the land around your well. A nitrate test is recommended for all wells. If the nitrate level in your water is higher than the EPA standards, you should look for other sources of water or ways to treat your water.

Volatile Organic Compounds (VOCs)

VOCs are industrial and fuel-related chemicals that may cause bad health effects at certain levels. Which VOCs to test for depends on where you live. Contact your local health or environmental department, or the EPA to find out if any VOCs are a problem in your region. Some VOCs to ask about testing for are benzene, carbon tetrachloride, toluene, trichloroethelene, and methyl tertiary butyl ether (MTBE).

Other germs or harmful chemicals that you should test for will depend on where your well is located on your property, which state you live in, and whether you live in an urban or rural area. These tests could include testing for lead, arsenic, mercury, radium, atrazine, and other pesticides.

You should check with your local health or environmental department, or the EPA to find out if any of these contaminants are a problem in your region.

Please remember that if your test results say that there are germs or chemicals in your water, you should contact your local health or environmental department for guidance in interpreting the test.

When to Have Your Well Tested

At a minimum, check your well every spring to make sure there are no mechanical problems; test it once each year for total coliform bacteria, nitrates, total dissolved solids, and pH levels. If you suspect other contaminants, you should test for those as well. However, spend time identifying potential problems as these tests can be expensive. The best way to start is to consult a local expert, such as the local health department, about local contaminants of concern. You should also have your well tested if:

■ There are known problems with well water in your area
■ You have experienced problems near your well (i.e., flooding, land disturbances, and nearby waste disposal sites)
■ You replace or repair any part of your well system
■ You notice a change in water quality (i.e., taste, color, odor)

Who Should Test Your Well

State and local health or environmental departments often test for nitrates, total coliforms, fecal coliform, volatile organic compounds, and pH (see above). Health or environmental departments, or county governments should have a list of the state-certified (licensed) laboratories in your area that test for a variety of substances.

For more information, visit one of the links below or contact your local health department or the EPA Safe Drinking Water Hotline at (800) 426-4791.

- Well Water Information Based on Where You Live (Environmental Protection Agency)
- State Certified Drinking Water Laboratories (Environmental Protection Agency)

WATER-RELATED DISEASES AND CONTAMINANTS IN PRIVATE WELLS

Over 15 million U.S. households obtain their drinking water from private wells, which are not covered by the United States Environmental Protection Agency (EPA) regulations that protect public drinking water systems. Although the United States has one of the safest drinking water supplies in the world, sources of drinking water can still become contaminated through naturally occurring chemicals and minerals (for example, arsenic, radon), local land use practices (for example, pesticides, chemicals, animal feeding operations), malfunctioning wastewater treatment systems (for example, sewer overflows), and other sources. Contamination of a private well can impact not only the household served by the well, but also nearby households using the same aquifer.

Owners of private wells are responsible for ensuring that their water is safe from contaminants. Private wells should be checked every year for mechanical problems, cleanliness, and the presence of coliform bacteria, nitrates, and any other contaminants of local concern. A local health department or water well systems professional can help ensure delivery of high-quality water from an existing well or, if needed, help locate and construct a new well in a safer area. Additional information about well maintenance and water testing is available at Healthy Water's Well Testing page.

The presence of contaminants in water can lead to health issues, including gastrointestinal illness, reproductive problems, and neurological disorders. Infants, young children, pregnant women, the elderly, and people whose immune systems are compromised because of AIDS, chemotherapy, or transplant medications, may be especially susceptible to illness from some contaminants.

The Top 5 Causes of Waterborne Outbreaks * in Private
Groundwater Wells

1. Hepatitis A (CDC, CDC-Water)

2. Giardia intestinalis (CDC, CDC-Water)

3. Shigella spp. (CDC, CDC-Water)

4. E. coli 0157:H7 (CDC, CDC-Water, EPA)

5. Tied for 5th:

> **Campylobacter jejuni (CDC, CDC-Water) and**
> **Salmonella serotype Typhimurium (CDC, CDC-Water)**

More well water-related pathogens and chemicals:

■ Arsenic (CDC-Water, CDC-ATSDR, WHO)

■ Copper (CDC-Water, CDC-ATSDR)

■ Cryptosporidium (CDC, CDC-Water)

■ Enterovirus (CDC, CDC-Water)

■ Lead (CDC-ATSDR, CDC-Water)

■ Nitrate (CDC-Water, EPA)

■ Norovirus (CDC, CDC-Water)

■ Radon (CDC-ATSDR, CDC-Water)

■ Rotavirus (CDC, CDC-Water, WHO)

For more water-related diseases, see CDC Healthy Water's Diseases, Contaminants and Injuries.

---

* Based on tracking of waterborne outbreaks from 1971-2006. Outbreak reporting is dependent on detection, investigation, and reporting of the outbreak. This requires health effects to be measured and these health effects to be linked to water exposure. However, many contaminants (i.e., many chemicals) in drinking water may not cause easily recognizable outbreaks because they require a long chronic exposure period. As a result, they would not be part of waterborne disease outbreak reporting or part of this Top 5 list.

PRIVATE WELL WATER AND FLUORIDE

This fact sheet addresses questions that consumers may have on fluoride levels in groundwater from private wells.

How do I know if my water is from a public water system or a private well?

The U.S. Environmental Protection Agency defines a Public Water System as a system that serves 25 or more people per day. If you have water service from a well that has a limited delivery, such as to your house but not to your neighbor's house, then you likely have a private well.

What are the governmental regulations for private wells?

Although most U.S. households are connected to a public water system, the U.S. Geological Survey report "Estimated Use of Water in the United States in 2005" estimates that 14% of United States residents rely on private wells that are not regulated by the EPA Safe Drinking Water Act. In most states, private wells are not regulated by governmental regulatory entities. Therefore, it is the responsibility of the homeowner to know and understand the quality of the water from their well. The U.S. Environmental Protection Agency suggests that all wells be tested for quality once every three years since influences to well water quality can change over time. Contact your public health office for their advice on testing of private wells in your state or area. Additional information on testing well water quality in private wells serving homes can be found on the U.S. Environmental Protection Agency Web site.

My home gets its water from a private well. What do I need to know about fluoride and groundwater from a well?

Fluoride is present in virtually all waters at some level, and it is important to know the fluoride content of your water, particularly if you have children. A 2008 U.S. Geological Survey study found that 4% of sampled wells had natural fluoride levels above the EPA Secondary Maximum Contaminant Level (SMCL) of 2 mg/L. A smaller set of

1.2% of all wells exceeded the Maximum Contaminant Level (MCL) of 4 mg/L. If you have a home well, the EPA recommends having a sample of your water analyzed by a laboratory at least once every three years. Check with your dentist, physician, or public health department to learn how to have your home well water tested.

What should I do if the water from my well has less fluoride than the recommended level of 0.7 mg/L? Can I add fluoride?

The recommended fluoride level in drinking water for good oral health is 0.7 mg/L (milligrams per liter). If fluoride levels in your drinking water are lower than 0.7 mg/L, your child's dentist or pediatrician should evaluate whether your child could benefit from daily fluoride supplements. (The prescription dosage of fluoride supplements should be consistent with the schedule established by the American Dental Association (ADA) Council on Scientific Affairs.) Their recommendation will depend on your child's risk of developing tooth decay, as well as exposure to other sources of fluoride, such as drinking water at school or daycare, and fluoride toothpaste. It is not feasible to add fluoride to an individual residence's well.

What should I do if the water from my well has fluoride levels that are higher than the recommended level of 0.7 mg/L?

In some regions in the United States, community drinking water and home wells can contain levels of naturally occurring fluoride that are greater than the level recommended by the CDC for preventing tooth decay. The U.S. Environmental Protection Agency (EPA) currently has a non-enforceable recommended guideline for fluoride of 2.0 mg/L that is set to protect against dental fluorosis. If your home is served by a water system that has fluoride levels exceeding this recommended guideline, but lower than 4.0 mg/L, currently EPA recommends that children should be provided with alternative sources of drinking water.

Continue to test your well water's quality every three years as recommended by EPA.

What should I do if my well water was measured as having too much fluoride (level greater than 4 mg/L)?

It is unusual to have the fluoride content of water exceed 4 mg/L. If a laboratory report indicates that you have such excessive fluoride content, it is recommended that the water be retested. At least four samples should be collected, a minimum of one week apart, and the results compared. If one sample is above 4 mg/L and the other samples are less than 4 mg/L, then the high value may have been an erroneous measurement. If all samples register excessive levels greater than 4 mg/L, then you may want to consider investigating alternate sources of water for drinking and cooking, or installing a device to remove the fluoride from your home water source. Physical contact with high fluoride content water, such as bathing or dishwashing, is safe since fluoride does not pass through the skin.

What are the health risks of consuming water with fluoride levels greater than 4 mg/L?

Children aged 8 years and younger have an increased chance of developing severe tooth dental fluorosis. Consumption over a lifetime may increase the likelihood of bone fractures, and may result in skeletal fluorosis, a painful or even crippling disease. The U.S. Environmental Protection Agency has determined that safe exposure of fluoride is below 4 mg/L in drinking water to avoid those effects.

Will using a home water filtration system take the fluoride out of my home's water?

Removal of fluoride from water is difficult. Most home point-of-use treatment systems that are installed at single faucets use activated carbon filtration, which does not remove the fluoride. Reverse osmosis point-of-use devices can effectively remove fluoride, although the amount may vary given individual circumstances. For a home point-of-use device to claim a reduction in fluoride, it must meet National Sanitation Foundation (NSF) Standard 58 criteria for fluoride removal. Standard 58 requires that a device must achieve a 1.5 milligrams per liter (mg/L) concentration in the product water if the original concentration was 8.0 mg/L, or approximately 80 percent removal.

This percentage removal may not be consistent at lower concentrations of fluoride. Check with the manufacturer of the individual product for specific product information.

Fluoride is not released from water when it is boiled or frozen. One exception would be a water distillation system. These systems heat water to the boiling point and then collect water vapor as it evaporates. Water distillation systems are typically used in laboratories. For home use, these systems can be expensive and may present safety and maintenance concerns.

Can I use water with fluoride for preparing infant formula?

Yes, you can use well water for preparing infant formula. It is important, however, to ensure that the well water has been recently tested to verify safety. EPA suggests that well water should be tested a minimum of once every three years for micro-organisms and other substances. In addition, parents of young children should also have their well water tested for fluoride content.

For more information on private well testing, contact your local health department or visit the EPA Web site. Parents and caregivers should speak with their pediatrician to review the results of the private well testing and to determine if the well water should be boiled prior to mixing the formula. If you are advised to boil the water, be sure to boil the water only one time so that you don't concentrate substances by the boiling process itself.

If your child is exclusively consuming infant formula reconstituted with well water, and if that water contains fluoride, there is an increased chance for dental fluorosis. To lessen this chance, parents can use low-fluoride bottled water some of the time to mix infant formula; these bottled water are labeled as de-ionized, purified, demineralized, or distilled. For more information, see Overview: Infant Formula and Fluorosis.

RESOURCES

American Water Works Association

Public Affairs Department
6666 West Quincy Avenue
Denver, CO 80235
Phone (303) 794-7711
www.awwa.org

Association of Metropolitan Water Agencies

1620 I Street NW
Suite 500
Washington, DC 20006
Phone (202) 331-2820
Fax (202) 785-1845
www.amwa.net

Association of State Drinking Water Administrators

1401 Wilson Blvd.
Suite 1225
Arlington, VA 22209
Phone (703) 812-9505
www.asdwa.org

Clean Water Action

4455 Connecticut Avenue NW Suite A300
Washington, DC 20008
Phone (202) 895-0420
www.cleanwater.org

Consumer Federation of America

1620 I Street NW
Suite 200
Washington, DC 20006
Phone (202) 387-6121
www.consumerfed.org

The Groundwater Foundation

P.O. Box 22558
Lincoln, NE 68542

Phone (800) 858-4844
www.groundwater.org

The Ground Water Protection Council
13308 N. Mac Arthur
Oklahoma City, OK 73142
Phone (405) 516-4972
www.gwpc.org

International Bottled Water Association
1700 Diagonal Road
Suite 650
Alexandria, VA 22314
Phone (703) 683-5213
Information Hotline 1-800-WATER-11
ibwainfo@bottledwater.org

National Association of Regulatory Utility Commissioners
1101 Vermont Ave NW
Suite 200
Washington, DC 20005
Phone (202) 898-2200
www.naruc.org

National Association of Water Companies
2001 L Street NW
Suite 850
Washington, DC 20036
Phone (202) 833-8383
www.nawc.org

National Drinking Water Clearinghouse
West Virginia University
P.O. Box 6064
Morgantown, WV 26506
Phone (800) 624-8301
www.ndwc.wvu.edu

National Ground Water Association
601 Dempsey Rd
Westerville, OH 43081-8978
Phone: (800) 551-7379
www.ngwa.org

National Rural Water Association

2915 South 13th Street
Duncan, OK 73533
Phone (580) 252-0629
www.nrwa.org

Natural Resources Defense Council

40 West 20th Street
New York, NY 10011
Phone (212) 727-2700
www.nrdc.org

International Bottled Water Association

1700 Diagonal Road
Suite 650
Alexandria, VA 22314
Phone (703) 683-5213
Information Hotline 1-800-WATER-11
ibwainfo@bottledwater.org

National Association of Regulatory Utility Commissioners

1101 Vermont Ave NW
Suite 200
Washington, DC 20005
Phone (202) 898-2200
www.naruc.org

National Association of Water Companies

2001 L Street NW
Suite 850
Washington, DC 20036
Phone (202) 833-8383
www.nawc.org

National Drinking Water Clearinghouse

West Virginia University
P.O. Box 6064
Morgantown, WV 26506
Phone (800) 624-8301
www.ndwc.wvu.edu

National Ground Water Association

601 Dempsey Rd

Westerville, OH 43081-8978

Phone: (800) 551-7379

www.ngwa.org

National Rural Water Association

2915 South 13th Street

Duncan, OK 73533

Phone (580) 252-0629

www.nrwa.org

Natural Resources Defense Council

40 West 20th Street

New York, NY 10011

Phone (212) 727-2700

www.nrdc.org

EPA Region 2

(NJ, NY, PR, VI)

Phone (212) 637-3000

EPA Region 3

(DE, DC, MD, PA, VA, WV)

Phone (215) 814-5000

EPA Region 4

(AL, FL, GA, KY, MS, NC, SC, TN)

Phone (404) 562-9900

EPA Region 5

(IL, IN, MI, MN, OH, WI)

Phone (312) 353-2000

EPA Region 6

(AR, LA, NM, OK, TX)

Phone (214) 665-2200

EPA Region 7

(IA, KS, MO, NE)

Phone (913) 551-7003

EPA Region 8

(CO, MT, ND, SD, UT, WY)

Phone (303) 312-6312

EPA Region 9

(AZ, CA, HI, NW, AS GU)

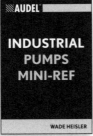